I0555241

U.S. Immigration Through My Eyes

My personal experiences involve illegal immigration, drug trafficking, human trafficking, and terrorism along the United States-Mexico border, as well as U.S. Ports of Entry.

by

Donald R. Smith

PREFACE

In my first book, "I NEVER SAW IT COMING," I outlined my forty-six-year career in law enforcement, detailing how I met my wife and how I got involved in law enforcement. It detailed all the places I worked and the locations where I worked.

My second book, "I Was A Police Officer," reflects my experiences as an Amite City and Baton Rouge City Police Officer. I discuss my experience working in the small town of Amite and transitioning to a large city police department in Baton Rouge.

This book will pick up from where "I Was A Police Officer" left off. I describe my work as a Border Patrol Agent on the United States-Mexico border and at U.S. Ports of Entry around the Country. It will illustrate my transition from a police officer to a federal agent. I discuss my experiences and attempt to clarify some common misconceptions about the southern border and the immigration problems it is plagued with.

I also discuss my experience working as an Immigration Inspector, Senior Inspector, and Area Port Director. This book will also cover the transfer of positions from the Area Port Director in the U.S. Virgin Islands to a Supervisory Special Agent in New Orleans.

I aim to write another book about my experiences, detailing each position I held, starting from a Supervisory Special Agent position to working as a Special Agent for Internal Affairs for the Department of Homeland Security, and sharing details about the various roles I served in.

Please understand that the information in this book is based on my recollection and the daily journals I maintained during this time period. Please visit my website at www.authordonaldrsmith.com for updates and information about my upcoming book, "SPECIAL AGENT."

Table of Contents

INTRODUCTION

In this third book, U.S. IMMIGRATION THROUGH MY EYES, I share my experiences working with the U.S. Border Patrol and serving in various roles within the U.S. Immigration Service. It also describes my time as the Area Port Director in the U.S. Virgin Islands.

In May 1988, I left the BRPD. I began my career in federal law enforcement with the United States Department of Justice (DOJ), working specifically with the United States Immigration and Naturalization Service (INS) and the U.S. Border Patrol as an agent stationed in Marfa, Texas.

In July 1989, I began working as an Immigration Inspector at Minneapolis International Airport in Minnesota for the INS. By May 1991, I had been promoted to Immigration Examiner at the INS Minneapolis District Adjudication Office, where I focused on investigating marriage fraud and other INS-related fraud cases.

In July 1991, I transferred to Houston, TX, to work as an Immigration Inspector at the Houston International Airport and Seaports. I handled criminal investigations and forwarded cases to the United States Attorney's Office for prosecution.

In November 1991, I transferred to Miami, FL, to serve as a Senior Immigration Inspector. My duties included prosecuting cases related to illegal re-entry and various other INS criminal violations.

In August 1995, I transferred to Atlanta, GA, to work as a Special Operations Inspector at Atlanta Hartsfield International Airport. I conducted secondary inspections, interviewed people trying to enter the U.S. illegally, and recommended prosecutions to the U.S. Attorney. In January 1997, I was promoted to Senior Immigration Inspector, where I handled criminal cases involving individuals who violated INS laws at Atlanta's Hartsfield International Airport.

In July 1998, I was promoted to supervisory immigration inspector in Atlanta. I supervised Immigration Inspectors at the airport who performed immigration inspections on individuals trying to enter the U.S.

In April 2001, I assumed the role of Area Port Director for INS in the U.S. Virgin Islands, specifically on the island of St. Thomas. I oversaw all INS programs on the islands of St. Thomas, St. Croix, and St. John. These programs included Immigration Inspections at all airports and seaports, Cruise Ship Operations, Criminal Investigations, Immigration Examinations, Immigration Adjudications, as well as Detention and Deportation Programs.

In June 2002, I joined the INS New Orleans, LA, field office as a Supervisory Special Agent. My upcoming book, SPECIAL AGENT, will detail my responsibilities in that role and my role as an agent working for the Department of Homeland Security, Internal Affairs Division.

CHAPTER 1

U.S. Border Patrol Agent

As I discussed in Chapter 5 of my first book, "I Never Saw It Coming," I was working with the BRPD when I decided in 1987 to pursue a law enforcement position with the federal government. I first applied with the U.S. Border Patrol (USBP) and the U.S. Marshals Service because, at the time, those were the only two federal agencies hiring. The one issue I had was that I didn't have a full college degree, as I was seventeen semester hours short of graduating with a bachelor's degree in criminal justice. Both agencies were willing to substitute the seventeen semester hours for my combined total law enforcement experience.

I recognized that employment in federal law enforcement would afford me excellent job security. Numerous federal agencies demand specialized training, thereby rendering their agents highly valuable. Additionally, I was aware that federal law enforcement agencies maintain field offices across the nation and in foreign countries. These locations would enable me to select my preferred place of employment and potentially facilitate transfers between locations.

Securing a position with the federal government took some time, as the hiring process was lengthy and the federal government moves at a slow pace.

Eventually, after completing the entire hiring process, I received a notice via mail that I had been offered a position with the USBP. I officially accepted the offer and was then informed that I would be stationed in Marfa, Texas, as my first duty assignment. I thought Marfa, Texas, where in the hell is that? I had to look it up because I had never heard of the place. Then I discovered it was out in West Texas, not too far from El Paso.

I was informed that before attending the Border Patrol academy, I had to first visit the Marfa Border Patrol Sector to complete the necessary Human Resources paperwork for employment and to tour the area where I would be living and working. Again, I explained this in detail in my first book, which makes for interesting reading.

In May 1988, I traveled to Marfa, where I spent a week on orientation, completing paperwork and meeting many people. Following this, I was sent to the Federal Law Enforcement Training Center (FLETC) Border Patrol Academy in Glynco, Georgia, to complete a twenty-week training program. The twenty-week academy was brutal, but very informative.

After graduating from the academy, I returned to Marfa to begin working as a Border Patrol Agent. My time as an agent in Marfa, along with working on the U.S.-Mexico border, proved to be an incredibly valuable experience. It opened my eyes to a new understanding of law enforcement.

Upon arriving back in Marfa, my first challenge was to overcome the culture shock again. Having spent years as a police officer, I suddenly found myself in a desert town surrounded by mountains and rugged terrain. I was completely out of my element and comfort zone and had to readjust entirely.

Understand that I was once a city police officer, fully immersed in urban life, where everyone spoke English and all amenities were readily accessible. I recall what I went through to be hired by the federal government. Before leaving the Baton Rouge Police Department (BRPD), I took pride in advancing my career, becoming a federal agent, and moving on to a more fulfilling and exciting life. I left behind my friends, family, and the comfort of a good police job. I took a leap of faith.

So, I prayed a lot. I asked God for a chance, an opportunity to make this new position work for me and my family. I prayed that everything would turn out well and that my wife, Linda, and son, Jacob, would give Marfa a chance. I had sacrificed a lot to get this position, but they had sacrificed plenty, too. They gave up their friends and the comforts of home to follow me. Linda left her mother, D-Dot, behind to follow me. I was under a lot of stress and pressure as I tried to adjust to a new job at a new location and learn many new things. I also had Linda and Jacob dealing with their emotions and the shock of moving to a new place like Marfa. Yes, the pressure was on me to make this work for my family and ensure everyone was okay.

Moving out to Marfa wasn't just about me; it's about family. How many spouses have been asked to give up everything and follow their partner anywhere? How would that feel? I wouldn't know because Linda never asked me to do that. But she could tell you what it's like, several times over.

The USBP

The USBP is responsible for monitoring and protecting international borders to prevent the entry of undocumented immigrants, illegal drugs, and human smuggling. Additionally, agents play a key role in identifying and stopping human trafficking and drug smuggling operations, and work closely with local and state law enforcement agencies.

Border Patrol frequently collaborates and shares resources with other federal, state, and local agencies, including the DEA, the FBI, the CIA, Immigration Investigations, and state police. We prosecuted many individuals who attempted to enter the United States illegally and posed a potential danger.

Our mission was to safeguard the American public from terrorism and related threats consistently. The men and women I worked with embody integrity, vigilance, and a strong commitment to serving the nation.

The Marfa Border Patrol Station covered about 4,500 square miles. It includes the northern part of Presidio County and all of Jeff Davis County, except for the section west of and including Chispa Road. To the south, Marfa Station is bordered by Ruidosa to the east, with ranch property fences marking the boundary with Presidio Station.

Marfa Station oversees more than 68 miles of the U.S.-Mexico border. The communities within the Marfa Station Area of Responsibility (AOR) include Marfa, Valentine, and Ft. Davis.

The communities of Ruidosa and Candelaria are situated along the Rio Grande, with only sparse populations on ranches in between. The total population within the Marfa Station AOR is less than 5,000.

Let me clarify that the southern border I worked on in the late 80s is not the same as the southern border of today. We faced issues with illegal crossings, drug smuggling, and human trafficking back then, but it wasn't as severe as it is now. I'll give you an example. My son played Little League baseball in Marfa, and I helped coach. We often traveled to Presidio, Texas, to play some of our games. Presidio is a small town in Presidio County, Texas, situated on the Rio Grande River, opposite the U.S.–Mexico border from Ojinaga, Chihuahua, Mexico.

When we traveled to Presidio to compete against a team from Ojinaga, most of the Mexican kids and their parents crossed the Rio Grande on foot and walked up the hill to the baseball field. The river at that spot was less than a foot deep most of the time. The Mexican parents brought their lounge chairs, ice chests, and small barbecue pits with them. I must say, the Mexican mothers cooked some delicious meals during the games. We all had a great deal of fun back then, and everyone understood one another.

After the game, they all packed up and began their walk back across the river. Everyone knew each other, and it was a family-oriented outing because they had brought their kids to play baseball. On a Saturday, we all understood that it was for the kids. Give them their day and have fun without all the foolishness of everyday life happening on the border. For that Saturday, I was not an agent; I was a baseball coach, and the Mexican parents were not crossing the border illegally; they were parents coming to watch their kids play baseball.

Today, that wouldn't be the case. It was a different era and setting back then, but honestly, those were good times. But as it's been said, it only takes a few to ruin it for the many.

Career Advancement

The career path of a Border Patrol Agent offers many opportunities for advancement within the agency. Some of the specialized units include the K-9 Unit, the Horse Patrol Unit, the Investigations Division, and the Intelligence Division, among others. These units offer unique experiences and the chance to contribute to specific areas of border security. Agents can progress to supervisory and leadership roles as they gain experience and demonstrate excellent performance. Promotions within the agency acknowledge agents' commitment and leadership skills.

BP Agent Duties

Agents inspect people entering and exiting the United States, seize illegal shipments, block the importation of weapons linked to terrorism, and monitor activities along the border.

Although the position can be dangerous and often requires working late hours, I was aware of these challenges when I accepted the position. I was fully aware of the dangers and welcomed the challenge.

From my first day of duty, I was introduced to national intelligence networks, worked with local law enforcement, and utilized military and law enforcement technologies. This was far beyond what I had experienced in police departments. I hadn't realized the extent of the technology that was available to federal law enforcement.

I remember my first actual working day as an agent. I mainly walked around, watched, and listened to everything, trying to absorb it all. I must have asked a thousand questions of my fellow agents. The senior agents were happy to explain things and show me how to operate specific equipment. Some of the younger agents were more reluctant to help. Honestly, from some of the younger agents that I worked with, they were a little reluctant to help because I believe they didn't fully understand it themselves. I guess they didn't want to show their ignorance. Not me; if I learned something and understood it, I shared my knowledge with my fellow agents who were new as well.

I learned about specialized equipment used to detect, identify, apprehend, and remove individuals illegally crossing into the U.S. Our equipment included fixed and mobile video surveillance, range finders, thermal imaging, radar, ground sensors, and radio frequency sensors, among others.

Since my time in the Border Patrol, this technology has been upgraded with ground radar, enhanced video, seismic and imaging sensors, and commercial location data to monitor near the border. Gaining knowledge of this advanced equipment was a valuable learning experience.

On an average day, I teamed up with an agent to patrol several ranch areas. Ranches around Marfa ranged in size from 9,000 acres to over 30,000 acres. After roll call, we retrieved the additional weapons we needed. Besides carrying our sidearm, we checked out an MP-5, a 9mm submachine gun that fires from a closed bolt. Military and police use this weapon because it is highly reliable, very accurate, and easy to control during use. Then we picked up a 12-gauge shotgun, all of our ammunition, and, of course, made sure to have plenty of water and food, usually canned goods, to take on patrol. The water was not only for us but also for those whom we come across in need. Keep in mind that our average day was ten hours, but when you went out, you never knew when you would return to the station. You had to be prepared for those possibly long overnight shifts.

After gathering our equipment, we planned our patrol route and updated the supervisor on duty so that they would know where we were patrolling. My partner and I often discuss scenarios and play them out in our minds, so that if something happened, each of us would know how to react and hopefully defuse any situation.

Our main goal was to prevent terrorists and their weapons, including weapons of mass destruction, from entering the United States along the southern border. Smuggling weapons across the border was common, just as common as smuggling drugs.

We also performed various other duties in addition to patrolling, which I will discuss in the following chapters.

Hiring Agents

When I started with the USBP, and even today, hiring agents to fill positions remains challenging. USBP is competing with other federal agencies that were also hiring. The issue was that you can't hire Border Patrol agents overnight. To become an agent, you must go through thorough background checks, and for good reason. Leaders of terrorist cells or drug cartels would love nothing more than to have some of their own working at the border! I can tell you that background checks can take months, sometimes up to a year.

Agents were required to undergo both security background checks and demanding physical tests, particularly during the academy training. Physical fitness in the academy was tough.

The southwestern border jobs were located in geographically remote areas, consisting of miles of isolated deserts and small towns. Not surprisingly, people with the appropriate law enforcement or military background to do this kind of work may not want to relocate to specific locations and bring their families to the border. You don't have a choice when you are first hired. The government offers the position and provides the location. You can accept it or decline, and you will then be moved to the bottom of the hiring list.

I understand that today, the Border Patrol is offering large bonuses to people willing to live in remote locations. I read a recent study that discusses the difficulties in hiring agents. A former INS commissioner, Doris Meissner, estimated that approximately twenty-seven candidates are needed to hire one agent.

Another reason for the lengthy hiring process is that applicants for Border Patrol agents are required to take a polygraph (lie detector) test. The study I reviewed indicated that 65% of applicants fail this test, which is notably higher than failure rates in other federal law enforcement agencies.

Currently, a Senate bill aimed at expediting hiring processes has been introduced. If approved, it would grant the USBP a three-year exemption from polygraph tests for applicants who have already taken one within the last ten years for any law enforcement agency. Border hiring challenges are expected to intensify with an anticipated increase in retirements in the upcoming years, which will likely exacerbate the workforce shortages. Again, the job is one thing, the living environment is another, and bringing your family there was another obstacle. It takes special people to do this job.

A U.S. Border Patrol Agent typically begins their career by completing an academy and then starts patrolling the Northern and Southern borders. After serving time and building seniority, you can transfer to other locations around the United States. Otherwise, you don't have to serve your entire career working at the exact location on the border.

Transfers can be requested, but preferred stations, such as those near the northern border, are typically assigned based on seniority. A point system determines eligibility for competitive transfers.

There are many programs available to help active federal employees explore transfer options to different locations or organizational offices at your current duty station. If you're considering relocating for personal reasons, you can request a reassignment through the Internal Placement Program or apply for a hardship transfer. We encourage you to talk openly with your supervisor and human resources staff about your preferences. Keep in mind, though, that approval isn't guaranteed, as agencies need to consider their organizational needs before approving any transfers.

Even if the agency isn't able to approve your request right away, there's still a good chance they might be able to help out later as circumstances change. Another great option for relocating is to look for open positions at the new location that are listed under the Merit Promotion Program (MPP) job announcements. This way, you can explore additional opportunities that might be a good fit for you.

CHAPTER 2

The Risks and Challenges

I want to emphasize that working for the Border Patrol entails several risks that significantly impact daily responsibilities. These dangers can be grouped into main categories, which are essential for anyone considering a career as a Border Patrol Agent.

Working as an agent in Marfa was lively and challenging in my view. We operated across different terrains and climates, from deserts to rugged mountains. We had to be ready to handle emergencies and various law enforcement tasks at any moment. Our hours were irregular, rotating shifts, and call-outs were always part of the job. Our shifts covered evenings, nights, weekends, and holidays. We had to ensure 24/7 border coverage to handle potential security threats.

We patrolled in remote and isolated areas, far from towns and civilization. The work setting demands resilience, adaptability, and the capacity to work independently.

The work we performed was not without risks. We encountered hazardous conditions, extreme temperatures, and dangerous situations during our patrols. One thing is for sure: we were committed and dedicated to protecting the border with unwavering resolve.

So, if you are considering being a Border Patrol Agent, you need to assess the risks to your physical safety. As I mentioned, we often worked alone in hazardous environments, which frequently involved threats from wildlife, extreme weather conditions, and challenging terrain. The physical effort required to patrol large areas on foot can cause injuries or exhaustion.

We faced almost daily challenges from criminal activities such as drug traffickers, human smugglers, and other offenders, which created serious safety concerns for us. We always needed to stay prepared for possible encounters that could turn violent and might lead to severe injuries or even situations that threaten our lives.

Additionally, you should consider the mental health challenges. Work demands can affect your mental well-being. Encounters with traumatic situations, like rescuing people from danger or dealing with criminals physically, may lead to stress, anxiety, or even PTSD.

Conducting interviews and interrogations with known drug smugglers, human traffickers, and domestic terrorists was highly stressful. The information we received from some of these individuals could keep you awake at night. I sat across from some very evil people during interviews who didn't care. They didn't care about their life, and they sure didn't care about yours.

During my police career, I interviewed some unsavory individuals and became hardened by some of the information I obtained from them. But after becoming a federal agent, the people I interviewed concerning drug smuggling, human trafficking, and human smuggling were extremely concerning.

It took me time to comprehend the mindset of some of these people. When interviewing evil people, I had to navigate a delicate balance between maintaining professionalism and effectively gathering the information I needed. Still, I had to conduct the interview methodically and respectfully.

Legal and political pressures often necessitate the management of complex regulations and policies, which can draw public attention and scrutiny from government agencies. This can sometimes lead to more stress and uncertainty for agents, making their work even more challenging.

Often, during efforts to arrest drug smugglers, we had to chase them, which occasionally resulted in gunfire. Sometimes, suspects try to shoot the patrol vehicle's tires, while other times, they shot directly at us.

Many times, suspects often resisted arrest and fought with us; some wielded knives or small handguns. During such confrontations, you risk being stabbed or shot. Also, working on or near the southern border often exposed us to extreme weather conditions. In the summertime, the heat can be unbearable. The winter was cold, with snow accumulating in the mountains.

Emotional Challenges

In summary, working as a border patrol agent involves facing numerous emotional challenges. These often occur in high-stress situations, frequently involving distressed individuals, which can be mentally draining and lead to fatigue. Witnessing violence and managing the consequences of illegal activities can also leave lasting psychological effects.

While conducting patrols, I often experience feelings of isolation and disconnection. There were instances where I spent twelve hours or more alone on patrol. The workload predominantly consists of administrative tasks (paperwork), which reduces opportunities for meaningful face-to-face interactions with colleagues.

Continuing my professional growth was essential to me. I took refresher courses and specialized training to improve my tactical skills and stay prepared for evolving security challenges.

Additionally, every five years, I was required to undergo a background check and a drug screening to demonstrate my reliability and integrity in law enforcement.

For those aiming for a career as a Border Patrol Agent, I found the job to be very rewarding. Besides serving your country, the work truly makes a significant and meaningful difference.

CHAPTER 3

Border Patrol Checkpoint

Occasionally, I was assigned to a checkpoint that was a permanent setup, featuring a small mobile trailer located beside the highway connecting Marfa to the Mexican border in Presidio, Texas.

The checkpoint was located about three miles south of Marfa, meaning that any vehicle traffic heading north from Presidio to Marfa had to stop there for immigration inspection. This road served as the primary route between Marfa and Presidio, and ranches bordered both sides of the highway. Upon arrival at the checkpoint, vehicles were mandated to pull over for an inspection by an agent.

Border Patrol checkpoints are inspection stations situated 25 to 100 miles inland from the U.S.-Mexico and U.S.-Canada borders. The checkpoints attempt to deter illegal immigration and various smuggling activities, including human smuggling.

Agents working checkpoints have legal authority that agents lack when patrolling areas away from the border. The United States Supreme Court ruled that agents may stop a vehicle at fixed checkpoints for brief questioning of its occupants even if there is no reason to believe that the vehicle contains people unlawfully present in the country. The Court further held that agents have broad discretion to refer motorists selectively to a secondary inspection area for additional questioning.

The Supreme Court held that agents on roving patrols may stop a vehicle only if they have reasonable suspicion that it contains people who might be in the country illegally. This is a higher standard than at checkpoints for stopping and questioning drivers. However, the constitutional requirement for searching a vehicle remains the same, and it must be based on either consent or probable cause, whether during a roving patrol or a checkpoint search.

The checkpoint had both primary and secondary functions. While working on the primary, if the agent felt that the vehicle needed additional inspection, it would be referred to secondary inspection. United States citizens weren't required to carry documentation, but lawful permanent residents had to present their Permanent Resident Cards, and nonimmigrants had to show their visas.

Our objective at the checkpoint was to identify, stop, and apprehend undocumented immigrants, alien smugglers, and illegal drugs coming into the country.

When a vehicle undergoes secondary inspection at the checkpoint, we question the occupants and verify their identities. Additionally, the vehicle is visually inspected for modifications that could hide drugs or other prohibited items.

I quickly learned how to identify drug smuggling activity, and after a few weeks of training and observation, I was given opportunities to engage in both primary and secondary inspections. My background in law enforcement was beneficial in this area, as it allowed me to communicate effectively with people and be observant when it came to narcotics.

Conducting thorough vehicle inspections was essential because overlooking any detail could have serious consequences.

Commendation Letters

Within the first three months of working at the checkpoint, I received three official letters of commendation from the Chief Border Patrol Agent in Marfa for apprehending narcotic smugglers coming from the southern border.

My first commendation letter was received on January 27, 1989. It involved an investigation I conducted that resulted in the seizure of 67.55 pounds of marijuana from a Chevrolet pickup. The marijuana was hidden in a fake gas tank located under the truck. Initially, the truck was escorted to secondary for further inspection of the occupants.

I interviewed the driver, who was a permanent resident of the United States. I searched around the truck for any abnormalities. When I looked under the truck, I saw that several metal screws were new and seemed out of place compared to the rest of the fuel tank. The new screws did not match the older ones. Naturally, the driver denied any wrongdoing and refused to cooperate with further questions. Based on the different screws, we removed the gas tank from the truck. After pulling out the tank, we found a compartment inside where the drugs were hidden. The fake tank was designed to fit inside the original fuel tank. It was amusing when we dropped the tank and opened it; the driver looked at it and said, "How did that get there?"

My second letter was received on February 21, 1989, and this case involved the seizure of 57.85 pounds of marijuana from a pickup truck. The truck was placed in secondary inspection for further examination of the occupant.

As I searched the truck, I noticed that the left rear taillight was very clean compared to the rest of the vehicle. The screws holding the taillight were also clean, with the screws being Phillips-style, including one flat-head screw. The driver admitted to having a quarter pound of marijuana in his possession, hidden inside the truck. I could tell his demeanor changed when we started looking around the taillight, becoming extremely nervous and talkative. I immediately grabbed my screwdriver and removed the screws, pulling off the taillight cover. I looked into the section and saw the marijuana hidden inside the left taillight section of the truck. The marijuana package had lemons cut up and wrapped around the package. I assumed he was attempting to conceal the marijuana odor.

The third letter was issued on March 6, 1989, and involved the seizure of 102.75 pounds of marijuana from a Chevrolet truck. The driver acted suspiciously, so he was sent to secondary inspection for further questioning. I noticed the right rear panel of the truck sounded hollow when I tapped on it. I went to the left side, and when I tapped the side panel, it produced a solid thump. The driver refused to cooperate or answer any questions. We removed the left rear panel, where the marijuana was hidden. It was stuffed and packed tightly, making it hard to remove from the vehicle. While trying to extract it, the bag tore, and the marijuana spilled out. We used brooms to sweep up much of what fell.

Working at the checkpoint was not challenging for me; I observed the drivers' body language, monitored for signs of nervousness, and documented their responses and reactions to my inquiries. This process represents a standard narcotic observation procedure for law enforcement officers.

Additionally, I could quickly determine if any modifications or alterations had been made to the vehicle. If something on the vehicle had been altered, such as a fender or light covers, I would notice it quickly. I learned that drug smugglers often did this to conceal their drugs in those areas. The problem for them was that when they either removed or replaced the part on the vehicle, the disturbance where it had been removed was visible. Usually, they would use either new screws or newer materials that, when completed, would look out of place for the type of vehicle.

Some drivers lacked common sense. A driver, about mid-twenties, pulled up to the checkpoint with both hands on the wheel while looking straight ahead. I observed the vehicle, which was a small light blue truck. I walked around the vehicle and noticed the left rear taillight area was clean, while the rest of the vehicle was pretty dirty. I asked him why that area of the vehicle was so clean. He looked at me, opened the driver's door, leaned out, and started to vomit.

Of course, he was sent to secondary inspection. The young man cooperated with us and told us where the drugs were hidden in the vehicle. Over a pound of marijuana was removed from that taillight area.

This individual became a victim of coercive circumstances. He became involved with undesirable individuals in Presidio while engaged in a game of poker. He incurred a financial loss and was unable to settle it at that time. Instead of monetary repayment, he was tasked with transporting marijuana through the Marfa checkpoint to take to Alpine, Texas, for delivery.

After we got him settled and calm, I interviewed him for over an hour. He provided helpful information about the individuals he was transporting the marijuana for and details on where to deliver it in Alpine. Without going into too much detail, we ultimately arrested four people from Presidio and two in Alpine. The driver was also arrested, but he eventually received probation for his assistance in the cases. He cooperated fully with us.

Human Smuggling

Sometimes, we also utilize a K-9 Unit to locate hidden individuals and detect the scent of drugs. Yes, many times, U.S. citizens have been paid to help smuggle people into the U.S. The ones they smuggle are usually individuals who can't enter the United States legally.

Smuggling people through the checkpoint was a rare occurrence. Most of human trafficking was done in large loads, usually in 18-wheelers on the interstate.

Human smuggling is the unlawful transportation of persons across international borders, frequently with their consent, yet contravening immigration regulations. Its principal aim is to facilitate entry into a country where such individuals lack legal authorization, often in exchange for a fee or compensation. Unlike human trafficking, which involves exploitation and coercion, human smuggling is typically consensual and centered on unlawful entry or transit.

This may include using a motor vehicle, aircraft, watercraft, or other means of conveyance to transport an individual with the intent to conceal the person from immigration or other authorities, or flee from authorities attempting to arrest or detain the person lawfully.

An example would be if a person charges a fee to transport undocumented immigrants across the U.S.–Mexico border. The smuggler uses a vehicle to move individuals through remote areas, attempting to avoid detection by border patrol agents. This act of transporting individuals in exchange for money, while circumventing legal immigration processes, constitutes human smuggling.

Smuggling can also occur when someone encourages or induces a person to enter or remain in the U.S. illegally, in violation of federal law, by concealing, harboring, or shielding that person from detection.

An example of this would be if a person provides shelter to undocumented immigrants in a hidden location, such as a basement or a secluded property, to help them avoid detection by immigration authorities. The smuggler might also provide false documentation and assistance in moving to other locations within the country, all in exchange for payment.

An example of this could be if a person supplies false identification papers, visas, or other travel documents to undocumented immigrants to help them gain entry into the United States. As an example, two men were convicted in federal court of conspiracy to transport migrants, resulting in the deaths of 53 people who were found in an abandoned tractor-trailer in June 2022, the deadliest known migrant smuggling attempt in U.S. history. Each man faced life in prison.

This was not the first instance in which these two individuals engaged in the smuggling of migrants. Reports indicate that they coordinated the transportation of migrants through shared routes, guides, stash houses, trucks, and trailers to reduce expenses and mitigate risks. They charged as much as $15,000 per individual for the journey.

The investigation revealed that the van lacked air conditioning and was operating in temperatures that reached 103°F. Several migrants lost consciousness, whereas others desperately clawed at the walls, attempting to escape. It was established that the 47 adults and six children who perished, along with an additional 11 individuals injured in the incident, originated from Mexico, Guatemala, and Honduras.

Before the incident, the two men allegedly acquired an empty tractor-trailer and arranged for a driver to operate it. One of them reportedly traveled to Laredo, Texas, to pick up the truck, which was loaded with migrants destined for San Antonio. When the members of the criminal organization encountered the truck after its three-hour trip, they opened the doors to find 48 people dead, including a pregnant woman. Sixteen individuals were taken to hospitals, where five more died.

Many migrants suffered from heat stroke and exhaustion, with no water available. The two defendants were aware that the air conditioner was broken but chose to ignore the risk to those in their care. There are many other cases like this one that occur, but mostly in smaller numbers of migrants.

The Mexican drug cartels often rely on U.S. citizens to smuggle people and drugs across the U.S.-Mexico border. After they successfully cross, they face checkpoints within 100 miles of the border. I will discuss the cartels further later.

Understand that smuggling groups were using U.S. citizens to avoid questions at legal ports of entry, knowing they didn't face the same level of vetting. United States citizens typically don't undergo the same level of scrutiny as foreign nationals. If the U.S. citizen is caught, prosecutors have charged the suspect with alien smuggling and operating an unlicensed money transmitting business.

As smugglers become more inventive and desperate, agents at crucial checkpoints use various techniques, including interviews and X-rays, to prevent illegal drugs from entering U.S. streets.

Marfa Sector also had an air branch, which was stationed in Alpine. They performed patrol flying small aircraft around the Marfa sector. Also, if you got into any danger, the air patrol could easily locate you and provide help.

CHAPTER 4

Checkpoint Secondary Inspection

Vehicles were sent to secondary inspection when the primary agent determined further examination was necessary. During the secondary inspection, I removed the driver and passengers from the vehicle to conduct separate interviews with them. In these interviews, one of them would often admit to having narcotics on their person or inside their vehicle.

Most drugs confiscated from individuals were purchased while they were in the Presidio. The drugs were commonly smuggled from Mexico into Presidio, and local dealers in the U.S. sold them. These were mainly small amounts of marijuana and occasionally small quantities of cocaine.

At the time, there was a zero-tolerance drug policy within twenty-five miles of the Mexican border. In other words, if you had a marijuana joint in your possession, you could be arrested at the checkpoint for a narcotics violation, your vehicle could be seized, and you would have to have a bond set. But honestly, I, like every other agent working at the checkpoint, was not there to target small amounts of marijuana for personal use.

If someone arrived at the checkpoint and was polite and cooperative, we would do everything possible to assist them. If it turned out that a person had a couple of marijuana joints for personal use, had no criminal record, and was a local or from nearby, we would have them destroy what they had right in front of us, and then they could go on. Hopefully, they will learn and never try to cross again with anything. Of course, we would make a report of the investigation to document the activity for future use if needed.

Our primary focus was on the quantity of drugs being smuggled into the U.S., rather than on drugs intended for personal use. We could have dedicated the day to cases involving small amounts of marijuana for personal use, but we decided against it.

Remember that sometimes, someone might approach the checkpoint with a small amount of narcotics, which could lead to their arrest and tie us up conducting our processing. During this time, a larger load could attempt to come through while we're occupied handling the smaller one. Using decoys was a common practice for drug smugglers. They did everything possible to deter, annoy, and tire us out.

Usually, only two agents worked at the checkpoint during each shift, with three agents sometimes on duty on Friday and Saturday nights. The team was small enough that if we caught a smuggler with several pounds of drugs, we relied on everyone's help to apprehend them.

When it came to actual drug smugglers detained during secondary inspection, some would cooperate and tell us where the drugs were hidden in or around their vehicle. Others wouldn't say anything, but when they use the narcotic dog on the scene, they tend to change their minds and become more cooperative.

I have to tell this story. A vehicle pulled up to the checkpoint. The primary agent placed the vehicle in secondary, driven by a U.S. citizen. It was a nice vehicle, but it reeked of marijuana. We knew he either had a good amount hidden in the vehicle or had just dropped it off at a location before reaching the checkpoint.

We decided to bring the drug dog out to walk around the vehicle, and when the dog started to search, the idiot kicked the dog in the face. I'm not going to go any deeper into this, but let's say he realized he made a grave mistake the moment his foot hit the dog's face. And I guarantee you that he most likely will never, ever, ever make that mistake again in this lifetime. The moral of this story: don't kick a drug dog in the face. They don't like being kicked.

Of course, he was arrested and charged with the offense. No drugs were found, but it was obvious that drugs had been carried by the vehicle because of the slight residue found. In the end, he did cooperate with us and provided information regarding drugs in the area. The information he provided confirmed what we already knew.

I could talk for days about the different encounters we had at the checkpoint. It was a fun place to work because the drugs came to you, and you didn't have to go looking for them. I couldn't understand why so many people carried and traveled with drugs, especially being so close to the Mexican border.

Drug Mule

One other aspect we encountered was "drug mules." Being a drug mule is a dangerous role in the illegal drug market. Some did it for the money, and some do it because they were forced.

These individuals serve as couriers, carrying illegal drugs for criminal groups, often crossing international borders, delivering drugs for higher-level traffickers. This role lowered the risk for the main organizers and distributors in drug networks. Drug mules usually have no other business with the drugs except getting paid for transportation, serving only as a link in the supply chain.

Drug mules use various methods to conceal and transport illicit substances. A common strategy is internal concealment, known as swallowing, wherein drugs are wrapped and ingested or inserted into body cavities. These packages are frequently retrieved subsequently using laxatives. External concealment involves affixing drugs to the body or concealing them within luggage, vehicles, or other objects.

People become drug mules due to a combination of personal circumstances and external forces. Financial hardship is a significant factor because the promise of quick money attracts those in poverty or with limited economic options. Some are coerced or threatened by criminal groups, making them believe they have no choice. Deception was also widespread; some mules were unaware of what they were carrying or misled about their destination. Drug traffickers will target vulnerable individuals, especially those lacking education or stable employment.

Choosing to become a drug mule is a risky decision. Efforts to combat this illegal activity should prioritize tackling the underlying reasons why people get involved, not just focus on apprehending traffickers.

You could always tell when a drug mule was caught, especially a new one, because they would often urinate on themselves. Their fear isn't directed at us but at the traffickers, fearing punishment, losing the drugs, and being stranded without money to go back. Someone always ends up paying, often with their life.

From the trafficker's point of view, the risks faced by drug mules are grave and potentially deadly. They risk severe injuries, such as internal harm from swallowing drugs and external harm from transporting them. Legally, drug mules face harsh penalties, including mandatory minimum sentences for drug trafficking. These sentences can range from life imprisonment to the death penalty, depending on the amount and specific circumstances of the case.

Fraud Documents

We often encountered individuals presenting fraudulent documents at the checkpoint. Most of these were fake permanent resident cards, also known as the old "Green Cards." The older cards had a plastic cover, which was often lifted to replace the original photo with a different one. Sometimes, they would even resemble the person on the card, hoping you wouldn't pay too much attention to it. These people were always the friendliest.

There was a young man who pulled up to the checkpoint with his car radio blasting. As he approached, he slowly turned the volume down while singing along to the music. He asked how I was doing and how things were going, and even asked if we were busy. He began talking about the weather, all the while bobbing his head, still listening to the song. He never once looked at me. He acted like he was in a great mood, trying to convince me that there was nothing here to worry about, because he had done no wrong.

When I reviewed his document, I noticed immediately that the picture had been altered or replaced. The document was a permanent resident card. He spoke decent English with a Hispanic accent. When I asked him to pull over into the secondary inspection area, his face started to droop, his eyes welled up with tears, and he became quiet as he pulled over to the secondary location. I asked him to step out of his vehicle, and he still did not make eye contact with me.

Of course, once the interview began, he immediately confessed to the drugs he had hidden in his vehicle and started crying. Sometimes, I couldn't help but step away and start laughing. Just a few minutes ago, he was a cool cucumber, listening to his music and thinking he could fool us. Now, he is standing there crying like a baby, confessing to everything. One thing is for sure: his head stopped bobbing, and of course, he started urinating on himself.

He admitted to having drugs in the vehicle, but it took a while for him to admit to the false document. He eventually admitted to having the photo swapped out for $500. Long story short, he provided us with valuable, detailed information, which led to several investigations, indictments, and arrests. He also had a pound of marijuana hidden inside his vehicle.

This particular guy cried so much that I had to have a long talk with him, telling him to start acting like a man and stop the crying. He eventually did, but did I say that he was in his mid-30s and lived with his grandmother in Alpine, Texas?

Some, like him, will tell you how much they paid for the document, but others will act like normal criminals; they never remember the name of the person from whom they bought it. It was like you were on the police force again, hearing, "I got it from the dude on the corner." I recall that as a police officer, if we could have caught the "dude" on the corner, we could have solved a lot of crimes.

I must also share this amusing story. One evening, while I was working the checkpoint primary, a small vehicle pulled up with two young white females. As I was inspecting them, they handed me two driver's licenses that, honestly, looked like they were made by a two-year-old. Both IDs were falling apart. So, I placed them in secondary to determine who they were and what the story was behind the IDs.

In secondary, I got them out of the vehicle and separated them so that I could properly talk with each one. I noticed the driver was seriously looking at the passenger, as if she were worried about what the passenger was saying. As I was talking with the passenger, she admitted that they were false IDs, and before she could say any more, the driver ran over and began beating the "crap" out of the passenger. Yes, two young, pretty women fighting, going to town.

We separated them, and the long story short was that the driver was getting married soon and had obtained fake IDs so that they could go to Mexico and have some fun. The fake IDs were used to avoid leaving a record of them crossing the border, as they did not want anyone to know about their trip. The last fling, I suppose you could say.

The driver said she did not want her fiancé to know, nor did she want anyone else to know. However, she said that when they reached the border, they lost their nerve and did not cross into Mexico. They stayed in Presidio and had fun there. She went on to say that she was worried we kept a record at the checkpoint as well, and she didn't want that.

We verified their identities using their authentic driver's licenses and conducted record checks, which confirmed that they were indeed U.S. citizens. They did not possess any drugs or anything illegal besides the fake IDs, which were enough. We had no choice but to charge them with presenting fraudulent identification. They ultimately pleaded guilty and each received probation.

The sad part is, these two women didn't realize how bad things could have been if they had been caught crossing the Mexican border with fake documents by the Mexican federal police. They would have been thrown into jail in Mexico, facing serious prison time. They were young, dumb, and reckless.

When all was said and done, their families learned everything that had happened during their trip. Both of them now have a felony conviction, and the last I heard, the wedding was postponed.

CHAPTER 5

Presidio County Sheriff

While I was stationed in Marfa, the sheriff was Rick Thompson, who strongly supported fighting narcotics in the county. Almost every day, he would pass our checkpoint, wave at us, and often stop to chat or drink coffee with us. Everyone knew the sheriff, and he was very well-liked within the community.

There were many times when he came up from Presidio, and most agents waved him through the checkpoint, so he didn't have to stop. We all knew him; he was the sheriff. No one ever suspected him of any wrongdoing. This guy was tough on narcotic offenders and always wanted to support Border Patrol. Everyone trusted him as the sheriff, and most of us called him a friend.

One thing that bothered me was the frequency of his trips to the Presidio area, which he made nearly every day. Sometimes, he would head south to Presidio in just his truck, and then, on the way back toward Marfa, he would often pull a horse trailer or assorted types of trailers. When he was pulling trailers, he wouldn't stop but blow his horn at us. No one paid attention to him. Now, I never said anything because he was the sheriff, and why would I suspect anything criminal? Since I was coming into Marfa from the outside, I was probably a little more suspicious than the agents who had been there for some time.

One day at the checkpoint, I asked several agents why the sheriff visited Presidio so often. Since Presedio was a small town with no sheriff's substation, it just made me wonder who he was visiting. All the larger cities were located north and west of Marfa, and we very rarely saw any deputy sheriffs heading south to Presidio.

One morning, I was fueling up my vehicle in Marfa when a deputy pulled up beside me to get gas as well. I started a conversation with him and asked how many deputies patrol the area in Presidio. He told me it was hardly necessary to go there because most of their problems were within Marfa and the surrounding larger ranches. I mentioned that the sheriff often goes down to Presidio, and he immediately said that the sheriff has friends there that he likes to visit. So, I finished fueling up and forgot about it. Those trips by the sheriff continued almost daily.

After I transferred from Border Patrol, I was working in Minneapolis when I learned that Sheriff Thompson was arrested on drug charges. Unbelievable!

The following information came from the Texas Standard newspaper dated January 15, 2016:

In the predawn hours of Dec. 3, 1991, a few miles from the border town of Presidio, federal agents said that a pickup truck with more than a ton of cocaine had forded the Rio Grande.

Those agents, it later turned out, had been tipped off by an informant. The next day, the then-sheriff of Presidio County, Rick Thompson, parked a horse trailer at the County Fairgrounds in Marfa. That trailer had been forfeited to the sheriff's office in a previous case. Inside that trailer? 2,400 pounds of pure cocaine, valued at close to one billion dollars.

The sheriff who had been a media darling in the war on drugs was later arrested, charged with drug trafficking, and sentenced to life in prison. "The quantity was really big, it was a lot of cocaine," says Assistant U.S. Attorney in El Paso.

The Assistant U.S. Attorney says Thompson's status as a law enforcement official is the key reason that he was sentenced to life. "You have to remind yourself it was in the early days of the war on drugs where everybody believed you could send a strong message and make drugs not be prevalent in American life."

Sheriff Thompson was a first-time offender. That alone might have mitigated the severity of a life sentence. However, he did something else that often staves off a life sentence, especially for a first-time offender. He pleaded guilty. And if you're going to get life in prison, you know, most people want to get something for pleading guilty and saving the gov't the expense of going to trial. So it was a harsh sentence for someone going up on a guilty plea.

Thompson initially denied the charge, claiming he was only transporting cocaine seized during a narcotics investigation. He has now served 24 years, and his sentence has been reduced to 30 years.

I share this because it shows that you never know. I guess I was once a narcotics agent and learned a lot about the drug trade and how people act around drugs. I internally knew something didn't seem right, but externally, I was influenced by those around me and their beliefs.

CHAPTER 6

Sign Cutting and Ground Sensors

As an agent, I learned sign cutting, which provides tangible proof of human presence through the environment left behind. I understood that anyone walking on the ground inevitably leaves a visible trace, like a footprint or some environmental disturbance.

The U.S. Border Patrol still trains its agents in sign cutting today, and even after the adoption of modern technology, sign cutting remains one of the most effective tools at its disposal for locating persons and gathering intelligence. Sensors and cameras can be fooled and rendered ineffective, but you might say that the sign never lies.

When you are sign-cutting, it is essential to consider bringing food, water, and an emergency blanket just in case you need to assist someone exposed to the elements. When tracking illegal migrants or criminals, you have to factor in your security. Illegals and criminals often do not want to be found and will sometimes attempt to conceal their tracks or improvise countermeasures to avoid detection. For this scenario, it was advised never to track alone. At a minimum, we carried communications gear for our self-protection.

Sign Cutting Tools

Sign cutting and tracking require minimal equipment. Besides food and plenty of water, we carried a good flashlight and spare batteries, even when working during daylight hours. Tracking operations can drag for hours in some areas, and what began as a morning look-see can easily become a night tracking operation. Sometimes at night, we would sign cut from our vehicle, which had a bright spotlight. We kept it at a low angle for better contrast.

Since tracking operations can drag on for hours, we brought basic sustenance items with us. As previously mentioned, we required water, food, a first aid kit, extra batteries, communication equipment, and any other necessary items. But we also tried to keep it light. Sometimes we ended up adjusting our load, making it a little lighter in case we had to get out of our vehicle and walk a while. When you are walking with your backpack and rifle, it can get cumbersome after a few hours.

Sign Interpretation and Tracking

Footprints give you clues about who you're following. You had to be able to interpret the footprints.

I realized that the size of the footprint usually shows whether I was tracking a man (larger, wider footprint), a woman (smaller, narrower footprint), or a child (small footprint). Additionally, the number of footprints provided clues about the number of people I was following.

The type of sole helped me stay on track when I encountered other footprints and allowed me to identify the person I was following. The sole could be from a tennis shoe, a cowboy boot, a work boot, or loafers.

Depending on the terrain, an individual may leave distinct footprints or none at all. Hard-packed and well-drained surfaces can hinder the formation of obvious footprints. In such cases, it is necessary to seek alternative signs. We looked for marks on the soil, such as scratches resembling coarse sandpaper. I looked for displaced rocks, with the moistened (darker) areas indicating recent movement. Additionally, I observed disturbances in the surrounding vegetation, including broken branches, snapped twigs, crushed or trampled plants, and displaced leaves.

I even looked for signs of clothing fibers stuck to vegetation. I was taught never to limit yourself to specific forms of sign. You should always look for other types of disturbances.

If we were patrolling on a ranch, it would be a good idea for us to walk it to determine how long it takes to travel across the area. When we did find a sign, this helped us decide whether to get out and track the sign on foot or try to leapfrog the sign and cut for it at another location, once we had chosen a direction of travel. It was good for us to know the ranchers and property owners in the vicinity. They were familiar with the area and could provide invaluable intelligence for us.

Our familiarity with the ranches and the surrounding environment proved advantageous in numerous ways. I acquired an intriguing technique for night tracking, whereby I learned to observe the insects in the vicinity, as they can serve as valuable indicators of the surrounding environment.

One night, my partner and I positioned ourselves in a location known for undocumented migrants passing through during the night. I was told to listen to the crickets chirping. After establishing our position, I focused on listening to those crickets. Were they chirping as they usually do, because if the chirping ceased, it often signaled the presence of animals or humans. This was quite interesting, and it turned out to be true.

During the sign-cutting process, we traveled through the mountainous areas around Marfa and headed toward the Mexico border along the Rio Grande. This journey allowed us to enjoy the scenic landscape and observe a variety of wildlife species along the way. I must say that the Marfa landscape was a beautiful place to see, and to be able to drive deep into the ranches was amazing. There were many hidden waterfalls and small ponds hidden throughout the region, and I was one of the few people who got to see them.

Most sign cutting took place on local ranchers' properties, each of whom provided us with a key to their gates, allowing us to drive in and out. The ranchers appreciated our presence on their land because they often observed illegal crossings in the desert area.

Ranchers often provide humanitarian aid to undocumented immigrants by offering food and water while out on the ranch. Many of these immigrants had been walking for days, running out of supplies and water. Water sources are usually accessible near windmills on ranches; these windmills, used mainly to water cattle, are scattered throughout ranches and at every farmhouse.

The ranchers' motives weren't always out of kindness to those walking through; they didn't want anyone to die on their property. I won't go into details, but numerous times, we found bodies in the desert and on the ranches of those who didn't survive.

Ranchers along the U.S.-Mexico border, near Presidio and Marfa, reported that their safety was at risk and that local resources were stretched thin. They blamed illegal migrants for causing severe financial strain and disruptions. Fences were sometimes cut as illegal migrants crossed their farms and ranches. Property was damaged, and trash was often left scattered across the land, creating a trail.

The ranchers also reported to the sheriff's office that their homes and barns were vandalized or broken into, and that vehicles and other equipment were stolen. They often found their tractors miles away from the ranch, driven by illegals until they ran out of fuel.

While patrolling the ranches, we often found clothes, backpacks, and other items left behind in the "camps" as illegal migrants moved through the property. Of course, the ranchers had to drive around their property picking up the trash.

If we found footprints or other signs indicating someone had been nearby, we would track them as far as possible to determine their direction. This process helps us identify the routes taken by illegal immigrants, enabling us to locate them for later apprehension.

Most people associate tracking or sign-cutting with following footprints, but it encompasses much more. It involves observing kicked-over rocks, soil depressions, clothing fibers, and environmental changes. The primary aim is to identify any disturbances caused by the person or persons being tracked.

All agents utilized sign cutting, which remains one of the most effective methods for locating individuals and gathering intelligence on drug and human smuggling.

During the summer months, patrolling ranches in search of signs proved to be a strenuous and uncomfortable task. Temperatures rose considerably, exceeding 120 degrees Fahrenheit, necessitating frequent hydration, often consuming water at an extraordinary rate. It was standard practice to pause at every windmill encountered to replenish water canteens, bottles, and any other available containers.

I was working for only a few months when I realized how vital water was to our survival. Before you know it, you could become dehydrated, very cold, and sick to your stomach. That's when you realize you're in trouble, and it's time to call for help.

One day, I was about fifteen miles or more from civilization and at least an hour before anyone could come to my aid. The last thing I needed was to be out on patrol, feeling bad, and then having to encounter four illegal migrants walking in the desert. I approached them, and they obeyed my commands in Spanish, but before I knew it, all four turned and attacked me, and I found myself fighting for my life. Thank God, I had enough strength during the struggle with one of the males to draw my weapon and press it to his head. This caused the other three to stop and back away. I was able to arrest all four, and they were charged with assaulting a federal agent and being in the U.S. illegally.

They were all eventually convicted of a felony, and after serving six months, they were deported back to Mexico. Not one had a prior arrest or prior entry into the United States. But now, if they get caught attempting to come back into the U.S., they could be charged as Re-entry After Deportation as a convicted felon.

Did the four men intend to kill me? I don't think so. I believe they would have only forced me into a situation where I couldn't chase after them, whatever that might involve. These men weren't murderers; they were just desperate. Still, I'm glad I didn't have to find out what they might have done.

Scenarios like this were common in the field. Most of the time, we traveled in pairs, but often you were on your own. You made sure to carry water, food, and stay in shape because being out there alone meant you'd face challenges.

Ground Sensors

The Marfa Sector also used ground sensors installed in the ground and hidden cameras placed in various locations across the desert and mountains. These sensors were set along previously used smuggling routes or on potential future routes. When someone walks on or near a sensor, it would alert the Border Patrol Sector. In response, an agent would be sent to that site to identify who or what had triggered the sensor.

Occasionally, an animal would pass by and step on the sensor. Upon arriving at the location, one could observe tracks left by either animals or human footprints.

Often, while patrolling a ranch or out in the desert, a sensor would alert in a particular sector. This could be at 1:00 a.m. or 1:00 p.m. As I drove to the location or approached the area, you might see six or more illegal migrants walking in a straight line, dragging a large tree limb or brush behind them to cover their tracks. Sometimes, they were glad to see you as you approached because they were running low on food and water. However, some would run, trying to make their way toward the mountains to hide. The issue they faced was that the mountains were several miles away. All you had to do was stay in your vehicle and follow behind them until they decided to turn around and give up. Either way, you would take them into custody and transport them in your vehicle back to the sector for processing and possible deportation.

Working at the checkpoint, responding to sensors, and patrolling ranches in Marfa was a terrific learning experience. I gained a profound understanding of immigration law and border law enforcement. The amount of knowledge I received opened my eyes to what the Border Patrol was attempting to do to prevent illegal entry into the United States.

We also employed surveillance systems, including sonar, infrared detection, night vision, and satellite imagery, to monitor activity along the southern border.

Who was coming?

I learned that in the 1990s and early 2000s, it was reported that an increasing number of single adults, usually males, were migrating to the U.S. for work. However, later, families with children started arriving, and they have different needs. While a single adult traveling alone may be okay crashing on a friend's couch, families often expect more for their children and may be more likely to need government services to protect them.

Today, communication has become more accessible, enabling migrants to effortlessly share information on social media regarding the most suitable destinations and available government services.

Many illegal migrants crossing the border didn't try to hide from the government. Some, upon apprehension, were granted humanitarian parole or received a notice to appear in immigration court. Once that was accomplished, they felt more empowered to ask for government assistance.

Years ago, most illegal migrants arriving in the U.S. were Mexican Nationals. Today, migrants come from a wide range of countries across South and Central America, Africa, as well as China and India. This diversity of origins makes deportations more complicated, as many individuals must be flown back to their country of origin.

In some instances, deportation was impossible because the U.S. lacks agreements with the home countries of its citizens, such as Venezuela. Today, this has changed.

Remember that a combination of economic hardship, violence, political instability, and the search for better opportunities in the United States causes most illegal crossings at the southern border.

Furthermore, Mexican nationals have endeavored to migrate to the United States for several decades. Historically, their primary motivation was to pursue economic opportunities, with the majority being young men traveling independently. However, in contemporary times, there is a noticeable increase in Mexican families migrating and seeking government assistance to sustain themselves.

Guatemala

Guatemalans made their way up through Mexico and attempted to illegally cross into the U.S. Extortion by gangs, poverty, and the effects of worsening climate change on farmers are all driving displacement in Guatemala and encouraging migration. At the time, most Guatemalan migrants came from the departments of Guatemala, San Marcos, and Quiché. The department of Guatemala, which includes the capital, has the fourth-highest homicide rate in the country and is an extortion hot spot. San Marcos and Quiché face widespread poverty and struggle to attract commercial activity and investment.

In Guatemala, increasing gang and cartel violence along the Mexico border has led to the displacement of residents. At the same time, reported climate change was affecting subsistence farmers, causing many to migrate north to the U.S.

Most illegal migrants who are apprehended go through a process called Title 8, which is part of the immigration law. During this time, they might be held or allowed to stay in the United States while their cases are being reviewed.

Asylum seekers were eligible to apply for work permits provided they attend court hearings and immigration check-ins. Some may need to wear electronic monitoring devices, such as ankle bracelets. Missing hearings or losing their cases can lead to deportation.

Apprehending undocumented immigrants at the U.S. border involved people from various nationalities. Most of the time, when you apprehended someone illegally crossing the border, even if they were found within 25 miles inside the border, they were usually Mexican nationals. These individuals were easy to process. Most Mexicans crossing illegally are doing so for the first time.

It's essential to note that whether a person crosses the U.S. border with a "coyote" (smuggler) or uses a counterfeit document, a foreign national who enters the U.S. unlawfully can face both criminal charges and civil penalties under immigration laws. Additionally, illegal entry can affect anyone looking to apply for certain immigration benefits in the future. The repercussions become increasingly severe if someone unlawfully enters the U.S. multiple times, or does so after a final removal order or having been convicted of an aggravated felony.

For the first improper entry offense, an individual may face a fine (as a criminal penalty), imprisonment for up to six months, or both. For a subsequent offense, the individual may be fined or imprisoned for up to two years, or both.

However, if that isn't sufficient to deter illegal entry, a different section of the law imposes penalties for reentry (or attempted reentry) in cases where the individual has been convicted of certain types of crimes, resulting in their removal (deportation) from the U.S.

Individuals convicted of three or more misdemeanors related to drugs, crimes against a person, or both, or a felony (excluding aggravated felonies), can face fines, imprisonment for up to ten years, or both.

Individuals convicted of an aggravated felony may face fines, imprisonment for up to 20 years, or both.

Individuals who were excluded or removed from the United States for security reasons shall be fined and imprisoned for up to ten years, and this sentence shall not be served concurrently with any other sentence.

Nonviolent offenders who were deported from the United States before completing their prison sentences shall face fines, imprisonment for up to ten years, or both.

What's more, someone deported before completing their prison sentence may be incarcerated for the remainder of the sentence, without any reduction for parole or supervised release.

Sleeper Cells

One more important thing to remember: there are those seeking to enter the U.S. for a specific purpose. These individuals are called sleeper cells. They are called "sleepers" because they lie low, avoiding suspicion until they are "activated" to carry out missions such as attacks, sabotage, or gathering sensitive intelligence.

Sleeper cells are covert operatives who stay inactive until called upon to carry out specific tasks, often linked to espionage or terrorism. These cells can present significant threats, especially during times of heightened geopolitical tension.

Recruitment efforts by these states associated with terrorism are generally conducted through networks, religious institutions, or online platforms such as social media. Recruiters often appeal to emotions, including feelings of alienation, injustice, or a sense of religious obligation.

Identifying these sleeper cells is extremely difficult. Some individuals who become sleeper cells are homegrown or enter the U.S. undetected.

Operatives are recruited by foreign governments, terror outfits, or intelligence agencies and are often rigorously trained abroad. These operatives migrate legally or illegally into the target country, sometimes using fake identities or visas.

They establish everyday lives, get jobs, get an education, build families, making them almost indistinguishable from law-abiding citizens.

Sleeper cells use encrypted messages, code words, or dead drops to maintain contact with their handlers. Once ordered, they may execute attacks, leak intelligence, or create chaos, often triggered during politically charged moments, such as wars or foreign policy escalations.

The phrase "sleeper cell" evokes images of covert operatives concealed within a society, awaiting the optimal moment to execute activities such as espionage, sabotage, or terrorism.

Although public perception often overstates how widespread and severe this threat is, the possibility that sleeper cells exist and could operate within the United States remains a primary national security concern.

Getting to know how modern sleeper cells operate is really important if we want to improve our strategies to fight against terrorism. These groups are quite complex and have become more skilled at staying under the radar, making it a real challenge to spot them.

Contemporary sleeper cells have an organizational structure that is highly adaptable and resilient. They typically operate within secret networks, which makes it challenging for law enforcement to monitor their activities.

A key feature of modern sleeper cells is their command hierarchy and compartmentalization. This structure helps them keep operations secure by controlling how information is shared within the organization. As a former intelligence officer pointed out, "Compartmentalization is a hallmark of sophisticated clandestine operations, making it challenging to identify the entire network."

Understanding how sleeper cells operate within society is essential. Sleeper cells are built to blend in smoothly with their environment, making them hard to spot and identify. They frequently live normal lives, holding jobs and maintaining relationships that give them a sense of normalcy.

Sleeper cells employ various integration strategies to evade detection. They adopt local customs and behaviors, facilitating their ability to blend seamlessly into the community and operate covertly. This level of integration is often so proficient that even their most immediate acquaintances, including friends and family, may remain uninformed of their actual intentions.

Some practical ways to integrate include creating a warm and stable family environment, securing meaningful employment, and participating in community activities to foster trust with local people. These steps help foster a sense of belonging and connection.

After the 9/11 attacks, the United States uncovered multiple sleeper cells affiliated with al-Qaeda and other terrorist groups. A well-known example is the Lackawanna Six, a group of six Yemeni-American men who were recruited by al-Qaeda and trained in Afghanistan. This group highlighted the challenges faced by law enforcement in identifying and disrupting sleeper cells. Although they did not directly participate in the 9/11 attacks, their recruitment by al-Qaeda raised concerns about the potential for future attacks on U.S. soil.

The Lackawanna Six were arrested in 2002 and later admitted guilt for providing material support to a terrorist organization. The case led to increased scrutiny of Muslim communities in the United States.

Law enforcement agencies have enhanced their cooperation and intelligence sharing to fight the sleeper cell threat.

CHAPTER 7

Mexican Nationals vs OTMs

While patrolling the southern border, we arrested various nationalities. Often, we encountered people in the desert who were Mexican Nationals who crossed the border between ports of entry. Most cooperated during arrest, and if they had no criminal record, they were processed and given a voluntary departure back to Mexico, and banned from entering the U.S. for at least five years. A voluntary departure was offered as an alternative to attending and participating in the deportation hearing process.

Most Mexican nationals took voluntary departure so they could return to Mexico and then try to cross elsewhere to avoid being caught.

If they reenter the U.S. unlawfully, they may face charges and imprisonment. They could be prosecuted under the law that covers improper entry by aliens. It states that anyone who enters or attempts to enter the U.S. at a location or in a manner not authorized by immigration officers, or who evades inspection, is subject to penalties. For a first offense, penalties may include a fine or up to six months in jail; repeat offenses can result in stricter penalties.

The law has also been amended to include penalties related to marriage fraud, with potential punishment of up to five years in prison and a $250,000 fine for those who enter into marriages to evade immigration laws.

We often encountered "Other Than Mexican" (OTM) individuals, who were not from Mexico but from numerous other South American countries, including those from China, Cuba, or the Middle East. These individuals were processed differently and were subject to a deportation hearing. The process took a lot longer, and apprehending 10 or more individuals tied up everyone on shift, and they were held in custody pending their deportation hearing.

Most Mexicans entering the U.S. were doing so for work, but not just along the border. Some individuals held permits to work and travel within a 25-mile radius of the border, particularly those employed on farms. They crossed at the Presidio port of entry, worked during the day, and returned home to Mexico at night.

Many Mexican individuals crossed the river into the United States to blend in, obtain false documents, and live without detection. Most would settle with family members already established in their careers and communities. They would use false documents, such as a driver's license, a social security card, and even a birth certificate, to establish a new identity, life, and job.

Mexican nationals with an arrest record who illegally crossed the border into the U.S. will probably change their names, acquire new documents, and start anew. At the same time, some of these individuals may not pose any issues while in the U.S., but others feel compelled to commit crimes. They are often caught and detained, and if found guilty, they serve time in U.S. facilities before being deported back to Mexico. The only way to get their true identity was to fingerprint them.

Before they were deported back to Mexico, they were fingerprinted and had their photographs taken. One thing they couldn't change was the fingerprints on their fingers.

There were occasions when we encountered an individual who attempted to have their fingerprints removed or severely damaged to prevent detection. But there were several other ways to obtain their true identity.

Many pregnant Mexican women often try to cross the border to have their babies born in the United States. When this happens, the baby typically becomes a U.S. citizen and can later file petitions for their parents to reside and work in the U.S. Then, the parents can petition to bring their parents and other loved ones to the U.S., where they can live, work, and potentially become permanent residents. This cycle can repeat, allowing each family member to eventually come to the U.S. But that's a complicated process to explain.

As previously mentioned, a large number of these individuals arrive, leading to the baby being born a U.S. citizen and thereby enjoying all related benefits. However, this practice also introduces several issues, including legal processes regarding the deportation of parents, concerns about the lack of regulation in the care given to the mothers, and allegations that some infants are being sold on the black market.

Border towns are overwhelmed by violent gangs, rendering them hazardous for all individuals, particularly those fleeing their countries with minimal possessions. This situation is especially critical for pregnant women. Numerous migrant attacks at the border have been documented; however, these accounts represent only those cases reported by victims or witnesses to law enforcement. Many cases never get reported.

That makes pregnant women some of the easiest targets for the cartels that menace, exploit, and extort migrants at the border because they tend to be among the most desperate and most physically vulnerable. There were incidents where women have been kidnapped, beaten, and shot by gangs. This violence, on more than one occasion, has triggered women to go into labor. Causing medical issues.

In some border towns, pregnant migrants encounter difficulties accessing basic healthcare because of factors like financial barriers, low awareness, transportation issues, and discrimination.

As previously mentioned, in the United States, Mexican women who give birth to a baby are generally regarded as having U.S. citizenship if the birth occurs on U.S. soil. This is based on the 14th Amendment, which declares that "all persons born or naturalized in the United States, and subject to the jurisdiction thereof, are citizens of the United States and of the State wherein they reside." Suppose the mother is unlawfully present in the United States at the time of the child's birth. In that case, the child may not automatically acquire United States citizenship, contingent upon the immigration status of the parents.

There were several occasions when a parent attempted to cross the Rio Grande River with a small child and got caught in severe currents, drowning both of them. This was not an uncommon occurrence along the entire Mexican border.

Then there were asylum seekers. These were people seeking protection because they faced grave danger in their home country. The hardest and first step they take is leaving their familiar environment, which means giving up everything they know, including friends, family, home, job, belongings, and safety. Many undertake risky journeys over land and sea to reach a safe place in a new country.

Even after an asylum seeker reaches their destination, safety isn't guaranteed until they receive refugee status. Asylum claims can take months or even years to process, and sometimes even longer if the right to seek asylum is suspended during crises. This has been the reality for hundreds of thousands of asylum seekers from Central America, Mexico, and Venezuela, who were turned away or expelled because of changes to U.S. asylum and border policies during the COVID-19 pandemic.

Although many countries are reopening their borders and resuming asylum claim processing, the path to asylum remains a challenging one. Ultimately, all asylum seekers aim to establish refugee status so they can stay in their new country, the U.S.

For many people around the world, the U.S.-Mexico border serves as a gateway to opportunity. Brazilians, Chinese, Pakistanis, and many others are joining the tide of Mexicans who sneak across every day. Once again, OTMs comprise individuals from diverse regions, including South America, the Middle East, and the Caribbean. Anyone who wasn't Mexican was considered an OTM.

As I previously mentioned, Mexican nationals were processed and deported within a few hours; however, Mexico does not permit the United States to return individuals from other countries to Mexico. Under U.S. law, these individuals are entitled to a deportation hearing. Sometimes, the immigration service lacked sufficient prison beds for all detainees. As a result, most OTMs were released and required to return for their court dates voluntarily, but many failed to do so.

They were issued paperwork called a Notice to Appear (NTA), which officially initiates the deportation hearing process. Unsurprisingly, reports indicate that very few people attended their scheduled deportation hearings. After they are released pending their hearing, they enter the interior of the U.S., obtain false documents, start work, and begin a new life.

Immigration Court Backlog

The next big challenge was tackling the backlog in immigration courts. With thousands of cases waiting, delays can become quite frustrating. Many immigrants found themselves waiting months or even years from the time they received their Notice to Appear (NTA) to having their hearing before a judge.

In states such as California, this waiting period can extend from two to three years. Meanwhile, courts are resolving far fewer cases than new ones are filed, which worsens the backlog.

I conducted research and discovered that there are currently 682 immigration judges on the bench. Due to the significant surge in migrants, the new average number of pending cases per judge is 4,500, which is an unmanageable workload for one person.

CHAPTER 8

A Man and His Mule

One evening, several agents and I conducted surveillance along a portion of the Rio Grande River. Intelligence information we received advised us that there was a possibility that an attempt may be made to bring drugs across the border using pack mules on this particular day and location. It was not uncommon for smugglers to use mules to haul drugs into the U.S. and then meet at a location to hand them off to dealers or runners. During this time, marijuana and cocaine were among the main drugs coming across the border.

We partnered up and, before nightfall, headed to the river to set up. My partner and I chose a spot with a clear view of the river, where the water was about 2 to 3 feet deep, shallow enough to walk across. We were sitting about 20 feet from the river. The other teams settled in different locations, about 20 yards apart. We sat in the area waiting to see if anyone with mules would cross the river.

By now, it was 11:30 p.m., and as we sat there, we heard a noise coming from the Mexico side. A Hispanic male came out of the brush with a small mule beside him. The mule had several brown sacks lying across its back. They started across the river, and as I began preparing to arrest him when he set foot on U.S. soil, my partner made me stop and sit down. He quietly explained that this man, accompanied by one mule, would not have any drugs with him. He was a spotter, coming to see if he would get arrested crossing the river without being inspected at a Port of Entry. If we arrested him, then the real drugs would not come to us. They will take the drugs to another location to cross. This man was testing the area to determine the location of the agents.

We sat quietly as the man approached us, leading his mule and passing within 15 feet of where we were hiding in the brush. What stands out most in my memory is the smell of both the man and his mule. It's an odor I'll never forget; it was so foul that it made me want to sneeze and gasp for air.

We watched as he and his mule passed by, continuing to walk north from the river. Our backup teams were positioned about a mile to the north, and once the man passed, we quietly radioed to inform them that he was headed their way.

We sat at our spot a little longer, waiting for the large shipment of drugs to come our way. Within an hour of the man and his mule passing us, I started to smell that same odor again. The wind carried it, and the scent grew stronger as the wind increased in speed. My partner told me that a bigger group was approaching to cross, and they probably had the drugs.

It wasn't long; we spotted several mules and four individuals staging across the river, preparing to cross. We waited, and about 20 minutes later, they began to make their crossing. At that moment, a crashing sound came from the woods behind us, as if someone was running. As the noise got closer, we realized that it was the man with his mule who had passed us about an hour ago. He rushed past us and returned to the river to cross back into Mexico. The people on the other side calmly turned around and started walking back into the wooded area in Mexico.

Things happened so quickly that we didn't have the opportunity to catch the one man who crossed illegally, and now he's back on the Mexican side.

We decided to leave and join other teams to assess what had happened. After speaking with the other teams, we concluded that the man probably saw the backup team before they noticed him, which led him to turn around and return to the river.

What I found amusing was the man's firm resolve not to leave his mule behind; he was tugging on it to make it move faster. As a result, we didn't seize any drugs that night.

I conducted numerous investigations involving criminal activity originating outside the United States. My role involved conducting interviews with suspects and coordinating with domestic and international law enforcement agencies to facilitate these investigations.

Deer Hunter

On one occasion, my partner and I went to the border for an initial reconnaissance mission. We searched for footprints to identify potential crossing points. It was about 3:00 p.m., and as we navigated through dense vegetation, we paused briefly to rest and drink water.

As we sat there talking, we heard a loud gunshot coming from across the river. We froze, trying to observe where it came from and to make sure no one was shooting at us. About five minutes later, we saw a Mexican male emerge from the woods, carrying a rifle. He began looking across the river, and eventually he focused on something, staring at it for a minute. He then placed his rifle up against a log and started wading across the river.

We eased down toward the river, and when the man stepped onto the U.S. side, we shouted at him to stop. He stopped and looked at us, pointing into the brush in front of him. We walked over toward him, and a small dead deer was lying in the brush, having just been shot.

Speaking Spanish with him, he told us that he had been hunting, and when he shot the deer, it had run across the river and died on the bank. He asked if he could take the deer home to his family. It was clear to us that he was deer hunting and posed no threat to us; he just wanted to retrieve the deer he had shot on the Mexican side.

We told him he could take it, and he grabbed that little deer and slung it over his back. He turned around and headed to Mexico. When he reached the other side, he looked back and waved to us, saying Thank you.

I, along with every agent, knew that the most important thing was that at the end of the day, you go home safely, relax, enjoy a nice dinner with the family, and get plenty of rest to do it all over again tomorrow.

As an agent, I was introduced to a world of law enforcement that was unlike anything I had experienced before, involving technologies and equipment I had never encountered. Working at the border was a completely new concept for me to learn and get familiar with. This type of law enforcement posed a challenge, focusing on identifying, deterring, and capturing undocumented immigrants, human traffickers, and illegal drugs by conducting surveillance from discreet locations at or near the Mexico border.

Being an agent also opened up many opportunities for me, and I learned about the various Immigration Inspection positions within the government. I researched the inspection program and found that these positions are part of the U.S. Immigration and Naturalization Service, just like the U.S. Border Patrol.

Another issue we encountered was finding deceased bodies along the banks of the river. Many were executed on the Mexican side and then dumped over on the U.S. side, leaving the U.S. to deal with it. Without getting into details, we knew from the condition of the bodies what we were dealing with. Most were individuals who were mixed up in the drug cartels and were executed.

My Personal View

As an agent, I encountered a diverse range of challenges and responsibilities that necessitated a combination of tactical skills, legal expertise, and robust ethical principles. My foremost duty was to enforce U.S. immigration laws, dismantle drug trafficking operations, and ensure the safety of the community. But the role was physically demanding, requiring operations in isolated and highly hazardous environments. These environments included threats from wildlife, adverse weather conditions, and challenging terrain. Nevertheless, despite these risks, I found the work to be highly rewarding while providing me with an opportunity to contribute to national security and public safety.

After speaking with Linda and weighing my options, I decided to proceed with applying to transfer to Inspections. I submitted the transfer paperwork for a role as an Immigration Inspector in the inspections program.

Not long after applying, I received an official offer for a position as an Immigration Inspector in Minneapolis. I will discuss this further in Chapter 11.

CHAPTER 9

Human Trafficking

Earlier, I briefly mentioned human trafficking, so I would like to clarify what it is and what it entails before discussing my transition to the inspections program.

Now, there are two types of trafficking to think about. You have human smuggling and human trafficking? What's the difference? Human smuggling involves illegal migration with consent from the person being smuggled, while human trafficking consists of the exploitation of victims through coercion or deception without consent.

For example, I will withhold the names and details of the individuals involved. A female was first trafficked by her parents when she was just four years old, and the exploitation continued until she was twenty-three. Everyone around her believed her life was normal, and she did as well. One day, she was able to learn the reality of her situation and escape from it. She was a sex slave.

Another female was abducted at the age of twelve while playing on the streets of Washington, DC, by a couple who sold her into human trafficking. She was sold to a man who took her to New York and trafficked her for many years as a sex slave.

I have encountered many human trafficking cases, and some were heartbreaking, especially those involving minor children. The issue is that children become used to the abuse and accept it as part of life. They were raised in the lifestyle and know no better.

Human trafficking is a serious federal crime with penalties of up to life imprisonment. Federal law defines "severe forms of trafficking in persons" as: "(A) sex trafficking in which a commercial sex act is induced by force, fraud, or coercion, or in which the person induced to perform such act has not attained 18 years of age; or (B) the recruitment, harboring, transportation, provision, or obtaining of a person for labor or services, through the use of force, fraud, or coercion for the purpose of subjection to involuntary servitude, peonage, debt bondage, or slavery."

In brief, human trafficking is a type of modern slavery. People who recruit minors for commercial sexual exploitation (or prostitution) break federal anti-trafficking laws, even if there is no use of force, fraud, or coercion.

There is no definitive profile of a human trafficking victim, as victims may be individuals of any race, color, nationality, disability, religion, age, gender, sexual orientation, or gender identity.

Human traffickers typically target people from poor communities, including children in the welfare system or involved in juvenile justice. This group also includes runaway and homeless youths, as well as individuals without legal immigration status in the United States.

Trafficking victims are deceived by false promises of love, a good job, or a stable life and are lured or forced into situations where they are made to work under deplorable conditions with little or no pay. In the United States, trafficking victims can be American or foreign citizens.

On numerous occasions, human smugglers (coyotes) have abandoned individuals during their journey through the desert. The smugglers depend on Border Patrol to locate and rescue these persons. Frequently, when approached, the individuals are willing to surrender, seeking sustenance and hydration. They also often declare asylum; however, their primary concern is relief and survival.

Individuals who commit these offenses may be either foreign nationals or U.S. citizens, including family members, partners, acquaintances, or strangers. They may operate independently or as part of organized criminal networks. Although it is a common assumption that traffickers are predominantly male, women are also actively involved. Perpetrators encompass pimps, gang affiliates, diplomats, business proprietors, labor brokers, as well as proprietors of farms, factories, and enterprises.

Human trafficking is a contemporary form of slavery that involves illegally moving people through coercion or deception for labor, sexual exploitation, or other profit-driven activities.

I was involved in investigations involving minor females who were being considered for prostitution and working in cleaning services, and other types of slave labor. These young females had no idea what was happening to them. I know that they were scared and often terrified of what would happen to them if they refused cooperation. So, they did as they were told, causing no problems. They knew that if they caused any resistance, family members could be harmed.

Additionally, they recognized that family members were getting money from their services. They chose not to interfere, understanding that the family depended on that income for survival.

Victims can be found in both legal and illegal labor sectors, including child care, elder care, the drug trade, massage parlors, hair salons, restaurants, hotels, factories, and farms. Sometimes, many victims are domestic servants within homes. At other times, they interact with people daily and are forced to work under harsh conditions in exotic dance clubs, construction sites, health and beauty services, or restaurants. These situations occur throughout the United States.

Certain factors, like poverty, increase a person's risk of trafficking. When people are desperate, they may sell themselves or their children to survive or accept work that quickly becomes slavery. A lack of good job opportunities often results in more exploitative work. Traffickers especially target migrants and refugees. Although these risks affect everyone, women and girls are more likely to face violence in trafficking situations.

Child trafficking

Trafficking impacts children every year, especially girls who are trafficked for sexual exploitation. According to the International Organization for Migration, family members are involved in nearly half of all child trafficking cases. Children from impoverished areas are most vulnerable, as their parents may feel they have no choice but to force them to work. Child marriage is a form of family-based child trafficking that affects about 1 in 5 girls worldwide, according to UNICEF.

There was a mom who trafficked her six-year-old daughter. For the next twelve years, the little girl was sold to men and was even recorded for child pornography films. She eventually escaped as a young adult thanks to the help of someone who recognized her situation and helped her.

Organ trafficking

Organ transplants among humans are frequent, but the supply often falls short of demand, fueling a black market for illegal organ trade. Vulnerable groups such as unemployed individuals, homeless people, and migrants are particularly at risk, as they may sell their organs out of necessity.

In some cases, traffickers trick victims about what's happening. In many areas, men are kidnapped for their organs or pushed by poverty to sell their organs willingly. Organ removal surgery is risky, leaving many unable to work or more vulnerable to severe illness.

The most harvested organs from victims of trafficking in persons are kidneys, followed by parts of the liver.

Forced criminal activity

When traffickers take control of a person, they often force them to commit crimes for them. This shifts the responsibility away from the trafficker and protects them from any liability. They aren't the ones committing the crime; it was their victim. Even if the victim is caught, the trafficker is in no fear of the victim talking or exposing any information. Forced criminal activity involves exploiting victims by making them commit illegal acts like street crime, begging, or drug trafficking. It also falls under labor trafficking, where individuals are forced to perform crimes against their will.

Victims sometimes find themselves caught up in all sorts of illegal activities that support criminal organizations. These can range from theft, growing drugs, selling fake items, to newer forms like fraud, which is often done through the misuse of technology.

Sex Trafficking Method

Many articles you read will portray sex traffickers as dangerous strangers, but in reality, most victims are familiar with their abusers. Many victims believe they are in a romantic relationship with the trafficker. This type of exploitation involves a trafficker grooming and manipulating a victim into an intimate relationship that may seem normal at first. Still, eventually, the trafficker coerces the victim into sex trafficking. Then come the threats of blackmail and violence, which are then used to keep victims trapped.

Human trafficking has been a persistent, ongoing issue. Some reports suggest that solving it is straightforward—by eliminating poverty. Since poverty is a primary driver of trafficking, ending it could significantly reduce the problem.

CHAPTER 10

Mexican Cartel

Before discussing the Inspections Program, I want to address the Mexican cartel, which has a significant influence on drug trafficking along the southern border. I'll keep it brief because I don't want to bore you, but I hope you'll stay with me for a short explanation.

Please note that this is my explanation. I do not consider myself an expert on the cartel; however, I have studied and participated in numerous investigations of various cartels, and I have seen firsthand what they are capable of. Literally!

To start, cartels are among the most powerful and dangerous criminal organizations, having become highly organized, violent, and sophisticated groups that exert significant influence over Mexico's political, social, and financial institutions.

Their origins stem from historical influences, political corruption, economic struggles, and the lucrative drug trade at the U.S.-Mexico border.

To understand why Mexican cartels hold so much power, you need to examine their historical roots, the Mexican government's involvement, the demand for drugs in the U.S., and the socioeconomic factors that enabled the cartels' growth.

The origins of Mexican drug cartels go back to the early 20th century, but they grew into a powerful criminal force in the 1970s and

1980s. During this period, several significant historical events laid the groundwork for the rise of the cartels.

During Prohibition in the United States, Mexican drug trafficking organizations emerged. These groups exploited the alcohol ban by smuggling liquor into border towns, creating early trafficking routes that eventually developed into drug smuggling networks.

After Prohibition ended, they didn't go away; instead, they turned their attention to marijuana and opium, which were both cultivated in Mexico. Cheap!

The 1980s signaled a shift in the development of Mexican cartels, notably with the emergence of the Guadalajara Cartel. Before the prominence of Mexican cartels, Colombian groups dominated global cocaine trafficking. However, intensified law enforcement efforts and military operations in Colombia prompted Colombian cartels to depend on Mexican traffickers to smuggle drugs into the U.S.

In 1989, the Guadalajara Cartel was dismantled under intense pressure from the United States. Its fall created a void that caused the criminal world in Mexico to split apart.

A primary reason for the power of Mexican cartels is the persistent demand for illegal drugs in the United States. The U.S. remains the top consumer of substances like cocaine, marijuana, methamphetamine, and heroin, all of which are trafficked by Mexican cartels.

In the 1980s and 1990s, cocaine became the primary drug trafficked by Mexican cartels. They quickly seized control of the cocaine trade, which helped them gain wealth and power. In addition to cocaine, methamphetamine and heroin were also involved. Meth production became a major source of income for the cartels. Because meth is relatively easy to produce, Mexico's cartels took advantage of this demand by smuggling large quantities of the drug into the U.S.

Don't ignore corruption, as it enables cartels to expand their power. The influence of cartels over Mexico's government, law enforcement, and military has been clear over the years. Many cartels have succeeded in turning Mexico's institutions into partners in their illegal activities.

Keep in mind that the Mexican police and military personnel receive low pay, making them susceptible to bribery. Cartels offer significant sums of money to gain protection, gather intelligence, or even seek help. These officers are frequently caught in a dilemma between accepting bribes and risking violent retaliation from the cartel. Consequently, many law enforcement officers either accepted bribes passively or engaged actively in cartel crimes.

Political corruption has played a significant role in strengthening Mexican cartels. Numerous politicians, particularly at the local and state levels, have been found on cartel payrolls. These cartels often sway elections by bribing candidates or using violence to threaten political opponents who resist cooperation.

Cartels and crime

To sum up, cartels and crime are closely connected, with cartels participating in numerous illegal activities such as drug trafficking, money laundering, human trafficking, and other criminal enterprises.

Cartels frequently bribe officials and elevate their members to positions of authority, thereby exerting influence over law enforcement and other institutions. This approach helps them maintain control and authority, often employing violence to assert their dominance over the territory.

The influence of the cartels extends beyond drug trafficking, impacting politics, law enforcement, and daily life in Mexico. They significantly affect the nation's security, economy, and social stability, thereby perpetuating a cycle of violence and corruption.

What will change? Nothing. I believe these issues will remain unresolved, allowing the cartels to continue exerting their strong influence.

Please note that my description of the Mexican cartel is based solely on my personal opinion, observations, and direct experience. It stems from what I have learned, studied, and the work I did with the cartels while serving in the federal government. While others might disagree with my overview, to me, it's just a summary.

CHAPTER 11

Immigration Inspection Program

On July 2, 1989, I became a U.S. Immigration Inspector in the inspection program. I left the small town of Marfa for the big city of Minneapolis. The move went well, and Linda and Jacob packed up, eager to try something new.

As I previously mentioned, in 1989, the inspection program was under the authority of the U.S. Immigration & Naturalization Service, Department of Justice. Today, it is overseen by U.S. Customs and Border Protection, a branch of the U.S. Department of Homeland Security. During my tenure in the Immigration Inspections Program, I held various positions, which I will describe in the following chapters.

After leaving the U.S. Border Patrol and transitioning into the inspections program, I took on various roles, including Inspector, Special Operations Inspector, Senior Immigration Inspector, Adjudication Examiner, Supervisory Inspector, and Area Port Director. I'll outline these roles, explain their objectives, and share some relevant cases I encountered in each position.

Working in the inspections program offered a valuable learning experience. I learned more about U.S. Immigration laws regarding foreign nationals attempting to enter the United States, as well as narcotics smuggling and human trafficking.

I quickly realized that being an Immigration Inspector required extensive learning and ongoing training. Despite my background in the police academy and the Border Patrol academy, the inspections program brought its unique challenges, with specific laws and procedures to learn and follow. My goal was to understand every detail so I could contribute effectively and support my fellow inspectors. I was required to attend multiple training sessions on interview and interrogation techniques tailored for the inspections program.

It didn't take long for me to feel ready to start investigating immigration cases. I discovered that studying immigration law, though fascinating, was quite complex. However, I quickly grasped the concepts and started learning easily. As I worked on more immigration-related cases, understanding everything became progressively simpler.

There is nothing like good hands-on training because I can stay in a classroom all day, but it's when I get involved in the actual cases that I start learning.

It's interesting to note that after American independence, there were only a few restrictions on legal immigration into the United States. It wasn't until the late 1800s that formal immigration policies were established. By that time, immigrants were generally considered eligible for permanent residence unless the government could specifically demonstrate that they belonged to a group considered ineligible for entry.

This presumption was overturned in 1924. Since then, all immigrants are presumed ineligible, and the burden has shifted from the government to the immigrant to demonstrate eligibility for specific qualified categories.

Today's immigration policy has some similarities to the early Chinese Exclusion Act, which also had its exceptions. However, unlike before, these days the restrictions are imposed on all nationalities, making it very hard for anyone to gain U.S. citizenship.

Duties of an Immigration Inspector

My role as a U.S. Immigration Inspector involved examining individuals entering the United States at designated Ports of Entry (POEs). A POE serves as a vital gateway for international travel and commerce, being the location where customs and immigration authorities inspect and process persons and cargo entering the country.

POEs manage the movement of people and goods across borders, enforcing customs and immigration regulations, and ensuring national security.

I was responsible for verifying the nationality and identity of all applicants seeking admission to the U.S. while simultaneously preventing ineligible foreign nationals, including those with criminal records, terrorist affiliations, or histories of drug trafficking, from entering.

U.S. citizens gain automatic admission once their citizenship is verified. Foreign nationals undergo questioning and have their documents reviewed to determine admissibility in accordance with

U.S. immigration law requirements.

The Immigration and Nationality Act (INA) authorizes immigration inspectors to question individuals entering the United States under oath to determine their admissibility. Additionally, inspectors have the authority to search a person and their belongings if there are grounds to suspect the presence of reasons for exclusion that might be revealed during such a search.

The INA is based on a principle of presumption: individuals seeking admission are considered aliens until they provide proof of citizenship; similarly, aliens are viewed as immigrants until they prove eligibility for a specific nonimmigrant category for entry. Several nonimmigrant classifications exist for individuals to enter the United States. A full explanation would require more space than this publication allows.

The mission of the immigration inspection program is to monitor and secure the United States' boundaries against illegal entry. As an Inspector, my responsibilities involve identifying counterfeit documents and fraudulent entry techniques to prevent illegal immigration. Additionally, I was tasked with pursuing legal action against those who attempt or aid in unlawful entry.

As previously stated, Immigration Inspectors examine individuals and their documents to determine if they are eligible for entry into the United States. An example is that a visiting foreign national, upon arrival at a U.S. POE, must present their passport and other required documents to enter the United States. You cannot enter the United

States until you have successfully passed through Immigration Inspection and an Inspector has placed an admission stamp in your passport. Only after these steps have been completed will you be permitted to enter the United States officially.

These documents are reviewed by a primary inspector, who is the first to examine and record the information.

Whether a non-immigrant or someone claiming U.S. citizenship who presents a U.S. passport, they are subject to secondary immigration inspection at a U.S. port of entry if the primary immigration inspector questions their admissibility.

Individuals may also be referred for secondary inspection if the primary inspector suspects they are smuggling contraband, violating customs or immigration laws, or committing any other federal offense, such as fraud or document fraud.

U.S. Immigration inspectors have the authority to determine whether a traveler can enter the U.S. or be denied entry and sent back to their home country.

At international airports, inspectors are responsible for monitoring the international arrivals area, which is separate from the main airport facilities and domestic flight zones. In this area, we handled foreign nationals arriving through the international terminal.

Interacting with people daily and questioning their reasons for visiting the U.S., I quickly learned to spot those trying to deceive or lie. Some foreign nationals attempted to conceal their true motives for visiting the United States. Most of them did this because they lacked the proper visa or intended to enter with malicious plans.

A Foreign National

When a foreigner arrives at a U.S. port of entry, they undergo a series of steps to ensure their admissibility. The process includes verifying the passport, confirming its validity, and ensuring that the appropriate entry visa is also valid. I would then inquire regarding the purpose of the visit, the intended length of stay in the United States, the location of accommodation during the visit, and the individuals to be visited.

Subsequently, I would compare the stated purpose of travel with the visa held by the traveler. When a foreign national presents themselves at a United States port of entry for an immigration inspection, they are requesting entry into the U.S. for a designated purpose and a specified period of time.

Please note that, like all Immigration Inspectors, I was trained and have considerable experience conducting immigration inspections for foreign nationals. I can easily identify individuals with a hidden agenda who attempt to enter the U.S. under false pretenses.

I asked questions to verify the identity and nationality of the foreign national applying for entry. Foreigners were often fingerprinted and photographed digitally during the primary inspection while at the counter.

If I were conducting a primary inspection and I identified any concerns during the initial inspection, the foreign individual would be referred to a secondary inspection area for further examination. I also had the authority to search luggage or personal devices (such as laptops or mobile phones) for evidence regarding the true purpose of the individual's visit.

The inspection process is designed to control and guard the U.S. borders against illegal entry and to ensure that all individuals entering the country are legally entitled to do so.

Airport Secondary Inspection

During secondary immigration inspection, the foreign national would be interviewed, typically beginning with the same questions that the primary inspector asked. Fingerprints will be rechecked to determine if the person has an arrest record or has been previously deported from the U.S. Then, the secondary inspector would be able to verify the story that the foreign national provided for the purpose of their trip. Once the story is verified and the person has a proper visa to enter the U.S., they may be permitted to enter the country.

Secondary inspection is significantly more comprehensive than primary inspection and may require several hours to complete. In most instances, a foreign national identified for U.S. secondary inspection is not considered to have been formally admitted into the United States.

If the secondary inspector finds discrepancies in the story and determines that the foreign national may have lied in some way, the person could be denied entry into the U.S. and be removed. Suppose the individual being denied entry agrees to a voluntary departure. In that case, they will be processed as a refusal and handed over to the airlines to be escorted out of the country. The airline is responsible for removing the individual from the U.S.

U.S. Citizen Inspection

If you are a U.S. citizen, the immigration process is substantially shorter. We would ask for your U.S. passport and verify your citizenship. We would inquire about your trip abroad and the places you visited, and then welcome you back to the U.S. After our inspection was completed, the U.S. citizen would proceed to U.S. Customs. However, U.S. citizens are not exempt from secondary inspection. If a flag is raised on a name or passport, the individual may be asked for more information about their trip abroad or life in the U.S.

Foreign National At a Land Border

When entering the U.S. at a land border, foreign nationals will be subject to the same general process. At land ports of entry, one immigration inspector will typically conduct the entire inspection process. This inspector may send the foreign national to a secondary inspection area to wait until he can continue the inspection process.

Arriving At A Seaport

The immigration inspection procedure at a seaport of entry closely resembles that at an airport. Foreign nationals who undertake a cruise in international waters surrounding the United States will constitute an exit from and re-entry into the United States.

Regardless of the trip's duration, travelers should expect to undergo inspection upon returning to the U.S. In most cases, immigration checks are completed before disembarking at a U.S. seaport.

There were instances where an immigration inspector would undertake extensive journeys offshore to rendezvous with a cruise ship and board it alongside the pilot responsible for navigating the vessel into port. Upon boarding, the inspector would initiate the inspection procedure and conclude it upon the ship's arrival at the seaport.

When I was in the Miami office, I conducted this procedure twice a week, meeting cruise ships coming from the Bahamas.

Legal permanent residents

The inspection process for a Permanent Resident, holder of a "Green Card," returning from foreign travel to the United States is inspected at ports of entry ("POEs") by an immigration inspector who determines their admissibility.

There are several ways a foreign national can apply for a Permanent Resident Card, also known as a green card. One significant way is to marry a U.S. citizen; other ways include employment.

As stated above, U.S. citizens are automatically admitted upon verification of citizenship. Still, noncitizens are questioned and their documents are examined to determine admissibility based on the requirements of U.S. immigration law.

All green card holders bear the burden of proving admissibility and may be searched without a warrant at any POE. This includes their cell phones, laptops, and personal property, which may also be searched. Permanent residents, even those who own property in the U.S., must maintain strong work and family ties to the U.S.

For green card holders who have spent significant periods outside the U.S., documentation showing their ties to the U.S. should be prepared and presented during secondary inspection. Documentation of this kind includes recent U.S. tax returns, evidence of ownership of a U.S. vehicle or a U.S. house, a letter from a real estate agency establishing a client relationship with the applicant, other significant assets, proof of family members residing in the U.S., proof of children attending school in the U.S., a residential lease agreement, and any U.S. employment.

After concluding a secondary immigration inspection, if we determine that an applicant has abandoned their lawful permanent resident status, they will be asked to sign a Form I-407, Record of Abandonment of Lawful Permanent Resident Status. Those who sign will relinquish their card status and then be returned to the country from which they arrived. They can then apply for a visa to come back to the U.S. to visit at the American consulate in their country.

Some applicants may refuse to sign the document, thereby relinquishing their status, and typically request a hearing before an immigration judge during the secondary inspection process. In immigration court, the government must prove, by clear, unequivocal, and convincing evidence, that permanent resident status has been lost through abandonment.

After the request to see an immigration judge, we would then initiate removal proceedings against the applicant and grant parole or non-immigrant status until the immigration hearing date.

Even if their green card is revoked or they sign Form I-407, the applicant may still request a hearing before an immigration judge to determine whether or not their green card status has been forfeited through abandonment.

Right to an attorney

Many people have asked me if they have the right to an immigration attorney during a secondary immigration inspection. An applicant seeking admission into the U.S. is not entitled to attorney representation during primary or secondary inspections unless they have become the focus of a criminal investigation and are taken into custody, or they request asylum in the United States based on credible fear.

Another question is whether a foreign national can request an interpreter if they don't speak English? That is a yes. A foreign national who does not speak English is entitled to request an interpreter, and we had a sufficient number of interpreters available for use. The airlines hired and provided interpreters for immigration inspections.

A Deferred Inspection

Let me provide you with a brief overview of deferred inspection. This process occurs when we temporarily allow a foreign national into the U.S. and then plan a more detailed interview at an immigration field office at a later date. It typically occurs when an applicant declines to sign an acknowledgment of abandonment of residency, and we decide on a middle ground between denying entry and admitting the applicant as a permanent resident.

It is used to conduct a more comprehensive interview and inspection. The applicant will be issued an Order to Appear – Deferred Inspection, which will specify the date, time, and location of the appointment. The appointment may be scheduled for a few days or a few months after the initial inspection, depending on the backlog at the deferred inspection office that has jurisdiction over the port of entry where the applicant seeks admission. A deferred inspection office was located at the district office.

At a deferred inspection, an attorney may be allowed to accompany the applicant at the inspector's discretion, but the attorney can't answer questions for the applicant.

There are numerous U.S. ports of entry across the country where immigration inspections help ensure that foreign nationals can enter and exit the country safely and lawfully. The United States thoroughly checks to make sure that everyone granted entry meets all the requirements and genuinely intends to follow the rules.

Marriage Fraud

During inspections, there are many other immigration violations to watch for, such as people coming to the U.S. to marry a U.S. citizen. If someone arrives in the U.S. to marry a U.S. citizen legally, they will have the proper visa, which will be processed accordingly. A person coming to the U.S. to get married without a marriage visa will usually lie, claiming they are visiting the country for tourism reasons.

After discovering their true purpose for coming to the U.S., we had to determine the purpose of the marriage. Are they entering into a legitimate marriage? If so, then we needed to investigate the relationship more thoroughly to verify its legitimacy. We needed to decide if it was a scam marriage, where the real aim was for the traveler to marry for benefits such as obtaining a "green card," which is a permanent resident card. At this stage, we focused on identifying the U.S. citizen involved and whether they participated in this arrangement for financial gain.

If a U.S. citizen were involved in a marriage fraud, they could face criminal charges. This might include requiring the traveler to testify against the U.S. citizen in a criminal trial and charging the traveler as well, before deportation.

Visa Fraud

Another critical aspect of conducting inspections was detecting cases of visa fraud. Many individuals try to enter the United States by using fake visas bought abroad in their home countries.

Individuals from Middle Eastern countries frequently attempted to enter the U.S. using fraudulent documents and visas. Sometimes, those fake visas were so convincing that inspectors allowed the individuals to enter the country.

I have reviewed many of these documents and visas, and they initially appeared to be in order. The only way to tell they were fraudulent was by taking them to secondary inspection and using exemplars and a microscope to examine the flaws.

In secondary, a book of legitimate visas and passports was available to use as exemplars. We could verify the visas and documents to determine if they are genuine or fraudulent.

Remember that U.S. Immigration inspectors have little leeway when it comes to interviews and interrogations. Individuals entering the U.S. at a POE, whether by land, sea, or air, do not have the same protections as U.S. citizens. They are subject to questioning to determine the purpose of their entry and their ability to support themselves financially during their stay. People from certain countries are scrutinized more closely depending on the intelligence information received.

For example, if intelligence reports indicate that one thousand visas from a foreign embassy have been stolen, then increased alertness would be in effect at ports of entry (POEs) to watch for these visas. If a foreign traveler from the Middle East enters with one of the stolen visas, you would examine the visa more carefully and scrutinize the individual using it. That person would then be sent to secondary inspection for further review, questioning, and visa verification.

We often prepared and presented visa fraud cases to the U.S. Attorney for criminal prosecution.

Foreign Students

Another example is foreigners entering the U.S. and claiming they are attending a school for higher education. Even though they may have a legitimate student visa, be aware that many cases prove they were coming to move narcotics from the border of Mexico or the northern border of Canada.

They would check into their school, attend a few classes, and then start missing classes because they were traveling. They would meet a person (the handler) smuggling drugs across the Mexico border and then transport the drugs to a person waiting for them at or near the school where they are enrolled. The student was the mule being used to transport drugs from the border.

You needed to be aware of the techniques used by smugglers and analyze how they relate to the student's entry. If you have doubts about the legitimacy of their entry, you should send them back to their country and not take any chances. You should remember the foreign nationals who came into the U.S. to attend flight school training. That turned into 9-11.

Working in the inspections program, I conducted twenty to thirty interviews each day. This experience helped me improve my interview and interrogation skills. Even before I started my academic studies in interview techniques, I was already developing my skills in facial expressions, body language, tone of voice, and overall demeanor. I was learning these skills on my own before I officially became aware of them.

I used to think I was a skilled interviewer, drawing on my years as a police officer, but my experience in the inspections program taught me even more. People from all around the world would come, trying to enter the U.S. through dishonest means, and it was my responsibility to prevent that.

Au Pairs

I have been discussing marriage fraud, visa fraud, and false claims to U.S. citizenship, among other issues. However, one of the biggest challenges we encountered during airport inspections was investigating cases involving au pairs.

Every day, I saw at least three or four young women trying to enter the United States at each airport where I worked. I worked at Minneapolis, Houston, and Atlanta airports, and the situation was quite similar everywhere. Many au pairs sought nanny jobs to earn some money, even though they didn't have the necessary visas.

I noticed that these young women lacked criminal experience; their youth and innocence made it hard for them to deceive. Dealing with similar cases daily helped me improve my ability to read facial expressions and body language, making it easier to spot lies. I also found that when I asked targeted questions, their answers were almost always consistent, which helped me become a more effective interviewer by paying close attention to body language and micro-expressions on their faces.

Why would they lie about coming to the United States? These young women wanted to come to the U.S. to work as au pairs or nannies for a family. An au pair usually lives with a host family, helping with childcare and household chores. In return, they get a stipend or allowance to cover their expenses and earn a salary.

Au pair arrangements are subject to government restrictions, which typically specify an age range, usually from the mid-teens to the late twenties. Young women considering becoming au pairs view this opportunity as a form of cultural exchange that allows both U.S. families and au pairs to experience and learn about new cultures. The issue was that these young women did not obtain the proper visas to enter and work in the United States for financial gain.

I was able to identify a distinct pattern in understanding these young women and their deception. When one recounted their experience, it typically mirrored those of other young women employing similar tactics.

A typical example is when a female foreign national appeared for immigration inspection and stated, "I am coming to see a family friend." Well, I've heard this story so many times that it almost always turns out to be false. Most of the time, they often say they've never met the friend they're coming to visit, even though the friend is allegedly a friend of their parents who wanted them to see the U.S. I would then ask how long they planned to stay, and their answers typically were, "Three months," which is consistent with previous similar stories. Everyone would have a B-2 visa in their passport, which is a visitor's visa, and if admitted, could be allowed to stay in the U.S. for up to six months. Most said three months, but they were hoping you would stamp their passport and allow a six-month stay.

When I inquired about their finances, they usually said they didn't have much money, but their parents would be sending them money. I also asked if they were enrolled in college; they always said they had taken a break from school.

Throughout my questioning, they never made eye contact with me. Their mouths often went dry, and they scoffed or smacked their lips as they struggled to speak. Usually, they would begin crying to seek sympathy, stating they didn't understand what they had done wrong or why they were being singled out. Occasionally, they would raise their voice to draw attention, thinking I would hurry and get them on their way.

When they started crying, I would let them sit for a while and then later ask them to share the names of the families they were visiting. Usually, they had to reach into their bag or retrieve the information from their luggage. There would always be a sheet of paper with the family's name, address, and phone number listed on it. Of course, I would have already gone through the bags and collected the necessary details. I wanted to see if they would be honest and truthful with me. But most weren't.

Searching through their luggage and carry-on bags revealed evidence of their true intentions for coming to the U.S. Many times, I found letters from the host family members in the U.S. confirming their employment and detailing the compensation they would receive. Some letters were from U.S. employers indicating the location of their employment interview and outlining the terms of their employment. I would gather this information and make a few phone calls to the employers, which will seal the young woman's fate. Employers will often admit to the issue once you inquire, as they do not want to deal with the potential trouble of a possible federal crime.

If the young woman were coming to stay with a family in that area, typically, the family would be waiting in the waiting area outside the airport's inspection area to pick her up. If they were going elsewhere in the country, I would need to make phone calls to the family about the young girl visiting them.

Once I obtained the family's names, I would go to the waiting area to meet with them and inquire about the young woman's visit. Most of the time, the family would be honest and say she was coming to help take care of the family in some way, but there were times when a family member would lie, telling the young woman she was coming for a vacation. Many times, I would have the letters to the female in my hand, and after I explained to them the amount of trouble they could be in for lying to a federal agent, they changed their tone and told the truth. They don't want to go to jail for someone they don't even know.

Most of the time, the waiting family would have a small baby or even have small children with them, and I would explain to them that I could not admit the young lady into the U.S., because she did not have the proper visa to enter and work. The family would explain that arrangements had been made for her to visit the United States, where she would work as their nanny and babysitter, earning a salary during her stay.

Some families explained that they had responded to an ad in a London newspaper seeking a young woman to visit the U.S. to work as a nanny in exchange for room and board and spending money.

After gathering all the pertinent information, I would deny the young female entry into the U.S. because the law states that one must be able to support oneself while visiting the U.S. and cannot seek employment during the visit. If you want to work as a nanny for a family in the United States, there are specific visas available that you can apply for to enter the country. However, these young females often try to bypass this process because obtaining a visa can take too long to meet their specific criteria.

Once admission was denied, the individual was processed for an immigration violation and offered voluntary departure from the United States. They were then handed over to the airline that had brought them to the U.S. If the individual refused the voluntary departure, they would be scheduled for an immigration hearing before a judge. It was the airline's responsibility to return her to the country from which she came when proceedings were over.

I never had a case where an au pair wanted to go before an

immigration judge. Everyone chose to take a voluntary departure and leave the United States. If they have appeared before an immigration judge and been ordered deported, they are barred from returning to the U.S. Therefore, they should return home and attempt to reapply at a later time.

I know that these types of cases may appear minor, but it's essential to recognize that they were attempting to enter the U.S. through deception and dishonesty. They were lying to a federal agent about all aspects of their arrival in the U.S. They were coming to work illegally and earn money from U.S. citizens without the proper visa and work permits. They could have been charged with a felony and banned from ever returning to the United States. We did not want to do that, and that is why we offered them voluntary departure.

Our goal was not to criminally prosecute these young females and ruin their lives, but we could not admit them either.

CHAPTER 12

Port Director Mike Conway

During my assignment with the inspections program at the Minneapolis office, the Port Director role was vacant until headquarters appointed Mike Conway as the new Port Director to oversee immigration inspections.

Mike turned out to be a great guy, and soon we became friends, sharing many activities both at work and outside of work. Although Mike may disagree, I believe he got the position only because I wasn't interested in it.

Remember, our team included Inspectors, Senior Inspectors, supervisors, and examiners, all approaching each flight inspection with professionalism and thorough preparation. However, there were times when we needed to relax, unwind, and lighten the mood. While taking our jobs seriously was essential, it's also natural to have a little fun from time to time. I want to share this story because, even though we take our jobs seriously, we also like to enjoy ourselves when we can.

Mike and I used to play pitch and catch with a baseball in the inspection area, known as the bowl, because of its large, bowl-like shape. It was a spacious room that could hold hundreds of airline passengers awaiting U.S. Immigration inspections. The ceilings were notably very high.

We played baseball games in the bowl between the immigration and customs inspectors, with some airport staff acting as umpires.

Mike and I consistently engaged in a competition to determine who was the superior pitcher. We would request one of the female interpreters or airport staff to serve as the umpire, responsible for calling balls and strikes while Mike and I pitched to each other. I would often attempt to persuade the umpires to call a pitch a ball if Mike threw a strike, thereby skewing the calls in my favor. However, I was unaware that Mike was similarly influencing the calls to benefit himself.

Those hardworking umpires (ladies) would sometimes become overwhelmed listening to Mike and me argue, so they would gently walk away to give us a moment to cool down, leaving our discussion temporarily unresolved.

Honestly, Mike was a sore loser, and I know he will read this, but it's the truth. Mike couldn't throw a baseball straight to save his life. I beat him in every competition. I was the champion!

Many days, we did more than play baseball. We would unwind by kicking the football around in the bowl area. As I stated, the bowl had very high ceilings, making it easy to kick a football.

One afternoon, while waiting for the 3:00 p.m. London flight, Mike and I started kicking a football around. Somehow, Mike kicked it so high that it hit the lighting fixture hanging from the ceiling, knocking it loose. It then fell to the floor, shattering glass everywhere. Coincidentally, the London flight arrived early, right at that moment.

We had to prevent the passengers from entering the inspection area while everyone worked on cleaning the glass off the floor. This caused a lot of stress for the airline personnel because of their connecting flights, but we did our best to remove the glass from the floor as quickly as possible. It was a total mess and an embarrassment for everyone. Nonetheless, Mike owned up to it like a man, and after the flight, we joked about it over a beer.

Mike never let much get him down, and he was always willing to have some fun, especially in the bowl area. He was also a great supervisor, and everyone enjoyed working for him. Mike had an excellent knowledge of immigration law and all policies and regulations concerning inspections.

Mike had patience with people, and he treated everyone fairly. I can't express how much I appreciate his willingness to be a mentor to me and others. Mike was an inspiring example of what it means to be a professional. He taught me many of the tricks of the trade, but he also showed me how much can be achieved with patient and gentle criticism. His passion was incredibly contagious, and I know that everyone loved working hard because it made us better at our jobs. The amount of support Mike gave us was immeasurable, which is why I will always strive to exceed expectations in everything I do.

Oh, I lied. He was able to throw a strike, but back then, I couldn't tell him that.

CHAPTER 13

Immigration Examiner

In May 1991, I was given the opportunity to transfer from the Inspections Program to the Examination Program, where I took on the role of an Immigration Examiner within the (Legacy) U.S. Immigration and Naturalization Service. This branch currently falls under the U.S. Customs and Border Protection, formerly known as U.S. Customs and Immigration Services.

I was assigned to investigate marriage and visa fraud cases by conducting extensive interviews with individuals who had been summoned to the office for questioning.

For example, I investigated cases in which U.S. Citizens married foreign nationals to help them obtain permanent resident status. This type of fraud occurs when two people claim to be married solely to obtain an immigration benefit, and at least one person does not intend to build a life together with the other, but instead is seeking a permanent resident card or another type of legal status. This can also result in serious legal consequences for all parties involved.

Some of the common cases I investigated involved individuals entering into a fake marriage in exchange for money or other benefits. Both individuals know that the marriage is bogus, and they agree to take part because one wants to get an immigration benefit.

Marriage Fraud

Marriage fraud in America is a serious crime involving marriages entered into for the sole purpose of evading immigration laws, often resulting in severe legal consequences for those involved.

Marriage fraud happens when people marry not out of love or companionship, but to secure immigration benefits like a green card. This form of deception undermines the integrity of the immigration system and poses a threat to national security. It is a federal crime, punishable by up to five years in prison and fines up to $250,000 for those found guilty.

Obtaining immigration benefits, such as green cards (permanent resident status), should be reserved for individuals involved in genuine, loving marriages where both partners intend to live together as a couple. If someone marries only for an immigration benefit, or if two people fake a marriage on purpose, this is marriage fraud.

Another form of marriage fraud is when a U.S. citizen gets scammed by a foreign national. What sets these romance scams apart from other types of scams is that, instead of an urgent appeal for immediate payment, the criminal moves slowly. They will communicate frequently, sometimes over weeks or months, to gain their victim's trust and make an emotional connection.

The scammer will mirror their target by saying, "Have you just lost a spouse?" So have they. Have you had any health problems? They have a treatment idea. By now, they have immediately captured the attention of their victims, U.S. citizens.

The scammer, by creating such an intimate connection, is essentially employing a classic scam technique, and it's highly effective. The scammer's goal is to steal as much as possible from the U.S. citizen victim. Unfortunately, elderly people often fall for this, and the scammer is rarely apprehended. Why? Because they are living in a foreign country and using sophisticated equipment to reduce the tracing of phone calls.

On numerous occasions, U.S. citizens have contacted my office to report that their spouse may have entered into a marriage to obtain a green card (permanent resident status). Now, they want to know what they can do about it. Discovering that their marriage may have been entered into for ulterior motives (obtaining a green card) was emotionally challenging for them and legally difficult. I could tell in their voices that they were truly upset about the situation and felt they had married for love. I explained that their allegation carries profound legal implications under U.S. immigration law.

After documenting their allegations in a report of investigation, I had to understand both the legal standards and the personal circumstances involved. U.S. immigration law, as outlined in the Immigration and Nationality Act (INA), requires a bona fide marriage, where the couple sincerely intends to build a life together rather than to secure immigration benefits.

Some fraud indicators included a lack of cohabitation, minimal financial interconnection, and/or discrepancies in their personal histories. For example, living in separate residences without a valid reason or limited knowledge of each other's details, such as family backgrounds or daily routines, will raise suspicions.

When assigned to investigate these cases, I examined the inconsistencies in documentation, including conflicting information on tax returns, rental leases, and utility bills. While doing this doesn't definitively prove fraud, it can prompt further investigation into the legitimacy of the marriage. Obtaining this information enabled me to conduct a thorough investigation to assess the legitimacy of the relationship, examine the couple's interactions, and review the documents they have submitted.

Conducting interviews with the couple enabled me to explore the personal aspects of their lives and confirm their shared experiences together.

Another investigative technique I employed was conducting an unannounced site visit to verify cohabitation claims, seeking evidence such as joint possessions, photographs, or interactions with neighbors. Any discrepancies I find may lead me to request additional evidence or conduct follow-up interviews.

A finding of marriage fraud carries severe consequences for the foreign national's immigration status. Under the I.N.A., fraudulent marriages result in the immediate denial of immigrant petitions, such as their request for permanent resident status, halting the green card process, and leaving the individual without legal status.

Being convicted of marriage fraud can also lead to a permanent ban from re-entering the United States. This type of fraud and misrepresentation could make the individual inadmissible to the U.S. for life.

Furthermore, those who deliberately assist with these fraudulent marriages, such as by submitting false statements or documents, may face criminal charges. This includes conspiracy to commit marriage fraud, which has similar penalties. My office actively investigated these cases to safeguard the integrity of the immigration system.

Impact on U.S. Citizen Spouses

U.S. citizen spouses can be charged with marriage fraud. If a U.S. citizen intentionally participates, they risk incurring criminal penalties, including fines and imprisonment. Even if they are unaware of the scam, they may be scrutinized during investigations, especially if they provide misleading information or fail to cooperate.

Financial obligations might also arise. If the foreign spouse received public benefits during the marriage, the U.S. citizen could be financially responsible under the affidavit of support they signed to bring the spouse to the U.S. This mandatory document requires repayment for specific benefits, even if the marriage ends or is declared invalid due to fraud.

Often, a U.S. citizen may arrange a marriage with a foreign national for financial gain, allowing the foreigner to obtain a status or benefit while living in the U.S. In exchange, the foreign national pays the citizen for their services. After the foreign national receives their permanent resident status, which usually takes five years, they may divorce, and the foreigner can then move on, retaining their permanent resident card.

I once investigated a case involving a U.S. citizen female who married and divorced three foreign nationals within a short period. Her main aim was to make money by charging them high fees to act as a surrogate bride. After marriage, she would sign as their U.S. spouse to help them apply for a green card. Once they obtained their green card, they would file for divorce, and she would move on to the next person.

Naturalization Certificates

I was also tasked with processing many naturalization applications. A Certificate of Naturalization number is a unique 8-digit alphanumeric number assigned to individuals who have been naturalized as U.S. citizens. This number is typically located in the upper-right corner of the Certificate of Naturalization and is printed in red on all certificates issued since September 27, 1906. It serves as a record of your naturalization and helps to prove your status as a naturalized citizen.

The U.S. issues a Certificate of Naturalization to a foreign national who has successfully become a naturalized U.S. citizen. It proves that the person named on the certificate has obtained U.S. citizenship through naturalization. The certificate confirms that the individual has all the rights and responsibilities of any other U.S. citizen.

Naturalization is the process by which a person who was not born in the United States voluntarily becomes a U.S. citizen. It is the most common way for foreign-born individuals to become U.S. citizens. This document is different from a Certificate of Citizenship.

When U.S. citizens adopt a foreign-born child, they usually submit the required paperwork for their child's naturalization. Once approved, the child becomes a naturalized U.S. citizen.

My position involved processing and approving many naturalization applications for adopted children. After completing the process, the family requested pictures of the child and me during our naturalization as U.S. citizens.

It is common for U.S. citizen parents to adopt foreign children and then have them naturalized as U.S. citizens, and the child would gain citizenship through their new U.S. parents.

While the children were too young to grasp the process now, they will someday look back on their naturalization, with me in the picture alongside them. It was truly an honor for me.

CHAPTER 14

Senior Inspector

I had many opportunities working in the inspection program and as an examiner, and one especially notable opportunity was serving as a Senior Immigration Inspector. I served as a Senior Inspector in both the Miami and Atlanta offices. The duties were the same at both locations.

As a Senior Inspector, I was responsible for investigating and presenting criminal prosecution cases from the inspection program to the U.S. Attorney's Office. These cases involved illegal re-entry after deportation, visa fraud, marriage benefit fraud, and false claims to U.S. citizenship.

On average, I presented numerous cases each month to the U.S. Attorney. The conviction rate was 100%, as most defendants pleaded guilty in exchange for being deported and returning to their home country.

Individuals who have been deported or removed from the United States face significant legal challenges if they attempt to reenter the country without permission. This statute criminalizes the act of reentry after deportation, and the penalties can vary based on the individual's prior criminal history and the circumstances of their deportation.

It was also common daily for a foreign national to attempt entry into the U.S. using fraudulent documents or a visa because they had been previously deported and were hiding this fact. These individuals would be prosecuted for re-entering the country after deportation and for possessing a fraudulent document. They would serve time in prison upon conviction and then be deported.

Then, there were cases involving individuals who obtained fraudulent visas and attempted to enter the U.S. illegally, which would result in felony charges. This is considered document fraud, which involves creating, altering, or using fake documents to deceive or mislead. Common examples include counterfeit IDs and forged certificates. Understanding the definition of fraud is crucial for identifying and combating this issue.

Document fraud involves a clever mix of digital and physical methods. Using sophisticated software, digital manipulation can softly tweak images or text, creating highly convincing forgeries.

Physical forgery is a hands-on process in which seals, stamps, or signatures are carefully replicated to create documents that appear identical to the originals. The method to use depends on the type of document and the level of conviction you need it to convey.

Fraudsters continually find new ways to exploit the latest technology to forge documents. They utilize high-resolution printers and scanners to create convincing counterfeit documents, and can even access official templates or graphics to make their fake items appear even more authentic. This makes it increasingly challenging for us to detect them.

In many cases, individuals attempted to enter the U.S. by

pretending to be a U.S. citizen with a fraudulent U.S. passport or by using someone else's U.S. passport to gain entry. Many of these cases were impostors. They swapped out the photo in a passport and placed their photo inside, or they may even look very close to the person's photo they are using. But fingerprints can't be duplicated.

Fingerprints are unique patterns formed by ridges and valleys on our fingertips. The belief that no two fingerprints are alike relies on the fact that the specific arrangement of these patterns, known as minutiae, is one-of-a-kind for each individual. Minutiae include features such as bifurcations (where a ridge splits), ridge endings, and dots, which can vary significantly even among people with similar overall patterns.

I communicated daily with the Assistant United States Attorney's (AUSA) office, submitting criminal complaints and affidavits. We vigorously prosecuted illegal migrants either for entering the United States without permission or for reentering the country without permission after a prior deportation or removal order.

Migrants are Prosecuted

Physical presence in the United States without proper authorization is a civil violation, not a criminal offense. This means we initiate removal (deportation) proceedings. Still, we do not charge individuals with a criminal offense unless they have previously been ordered deported and reentered the country in violation of that order.

If someone enters the United States on a valid visa and stays longer than allowed, they may face removal proceedings. Still, they are not charged with federal criminal offenses solely for this civil violation. However, those who enter or reenter the United States without permission face criminal charges.

Title 8 of the U.S. Code outlines federal criminal offenses related to immigration and nationality, including the following two entry-related violations.

Illegal Entry (8 U.S.C. 1325) makes it a crime to enter the United States unlawfully. It applies to individuals who do not undergo proper inspection at a port of entry, such as those who enter between ports of entry, evade examination or inspection, or make false statements while entering or attempting to enter. A first offense is a misdemeanor punishable by a fine, up to six months in prison, or both.

Illegal Re-Entry (8 U.S.C. 1326) makes it a crime to re-enter unlawfully, attempt to re-enter unlawfully, or be found in the United States after having been deported, ordered removed, or denied admission. This crime is punishable as a felony with a maximum sentence of two years in prison. Higher penalties apply if the person was previously removed after having been convicted of certain crimes: up to 10 years for a single felony conviction (excluding aggravated felony convictions) or three misdemeanor convictions involving drugs or crimes against a person, and up to 20 years for an aggravated felony conviction.

People accused of entry-related crimes have the right to a lawyer, provided by the U.S. government if they cannot afford private counsel.

However, in mass prosecutions, the quality of legal representation often declines due to the hurried nature of the process. Tens of thousands of migrants and asylum seekers are prosecuted for these crimes every year.

As a Senior Inspector, I regularly compiled monthly prosecution statistics and intelligence reports for both the Port Director of the U.S. Immigration Eastern Region Office in Burlington, VT, and U.S. Immigration Headquarters in Washington, D.C.

In criminal investigations, I collected evidence, documents, and other materials for analysis by our Forensic Document Laboratory in Washington, DC. I also testified before a Grand Jury and appeared in trials before federal judges and juries to assess the guilt or innocence of criminal aliens.

My investigations required strong interview and interrogation skills. Interviewing foreign nationals about their crimes was especially difficult because their mindset differed from ours. Many were unaware of their actions, seeing no alternatives; it's a matter of life or death for them and sometimes their families.

Many individuals I interviewed shared stories about organized crime syndicates forcing them to come to the U.S. to obtain employment and send money back to them. Young males and females would be separated from their families by the cartel in their countries and be provided false documents to get into the U.S. and seek employment. The individual would be forced to work to pay money to the cartel before they could send a portion of the money to their families.

Most males were guided toward construction work, and the females were guided toward prostitution. If they successfully enter the U.S., they will work and make their payments, ensuring that no harm comes to their family back home.

I will not delve into specific details; however, a strategic plan was tailored for individuals in such circumstances. This plan entailed regulating access, securing employment opportunities to generate income, and monitoring the transfer of funds, alongside conducting investigations within the country to locate the cartel. Naturally, all activities were undertaken with the cooperation of the foreign government and with the utmost security measures.

I gained tremendous experience working as a senior inspector, conducting criminal investigations. This position also allowed me to gain recognition from management for my strong work ethic and ability to successfully prosecute criminal aliens. This, in turn, enabled me to seek promotions and advance my career.

CHAPTER 15

Supervisory Immigration Inspector

Working inspections was great, whether as an Inspector, Senior Inspector, or Examiner. All were great opportunities for me, and I learned a great deal from working in those positions. But as in everything else, I always had a desire to progress and learn more.

Whenever I had the opportunity to obtain promotions and upgrades, I seized them. I was always willing to learn new things and take on new positions, and I wasn't afraid to jump in and try anything. Richard Branson is credited with the quote: "If somebody offers you an amazing opportunity but you are not sure you can do it, say yes – then learn how to do it later!" Well, that's me!

Supervisory Inspector

While working as a Senior Inspector in Atlanta, the Port Director for Immigration offered me a Supervisory Inspector position. After speaking with me for a while, he asked if this was something I could do and be comfortable with.

I was a worker bee and loved getting into the thick of things, so taking a supervisory position will allow me to supervise those doing what I loved to do. I knew that if I wanted to move up and try new things, I had to take those next steps.

I wondered if I could supervise and provide guidance to the inspectors and senior inspectors without getting too deeply involved in their cases.

After carefully considering the position and discussing it with Linda, I accepted the position.

On July 19, 1998, I was appointed as a Supervisory Immigration Inspector in Atlanta, marking the beginning of the next chapter in my career.

I supervised the inspection program in Atlanta, making decisions on the admissibility of arriving passengers and preparing work schedules while managing all immigration-related issues that arose at the airport.

I also evaluated the work performance of all the immigration inspectors and issued yearly appraisals. I also supervised the Senior Inspector Program, which involved scheduling assignments and managing criminal immigration cases for prosecution. I evaluated the work performance of the three senior inspectors and monitored their caseloads, which included instances involving detained individuals in jail. I assisted the senior inspectors in preparing their criminal complaints and sworn statements for prosecution. I often trained the senior inspectors regarding interview techniques, report writing, and intelligence gathering.

Training was a constant, and I attended sessions on Solving Performance and Conduct Problems, sexual harassment, Taking Disciplinary Action, EEO Training, Basic Labor Relationship Training, and Employer Sanctions Training.

I was declared an expert in the federal court system regarding cases that appeared in secondary inspection, such as Removals, Withdrawals, Credible Fear cases, Paroles, Cuban cases, and assorted Waivers.

As the Supervisory Inspector, I was occasionally asked to serve as the Acting Assistant Port Director for the Atlanta office.

I was involved in almost all of the criminal cases presented to the Assistant U.S. Attorney. I also continued to receive extensive training in interview and interrogation techniques, which I found beneficial.

As the Supervisory Inspector, I had the opportunity to meet many interesting people. One afternoon, I was notified that Roger Moore (James Bond) was coming to immigration for inspection. I was asked to meet him and get him through so he would not be hassled by the other passengers. When his flight arrived, I escorted him and his friend to our immigration office. There, I conducted the inspection and reviewed their visas and passports.

After completing their inspection, he asked me if there was a place to wait before his next flight, as he had a two-hour wait. The airlines offered him special services, but he preferred not to use them. Instead, he asked to wait somewhere quieter, so I took him and his friend to my office, where they sat and waited.

During that time, they made numerous phone calls and spent time in my office. I checked on them, and he invited me to sit and talk with him. I was slightly intimidated, feeling like I was talking to James Bond, and found myself staring instead of speaking. He told me to ask any questions I had. I asked a few trivial questions, which he answered, but

I couldn't help feeling I was sitting across from James Bond himself. He shared that he enjoyed playing Bond in movies but eventually wanted to explore other roles.

We had a pleasant conversation, and I was amazed by how polite he was. I made sure he boarded his connecting flight without any issues. Now, when I watch a Bond movie with Moore, I can say I met James Bond in person.

Many celebrities came through the airports, and I had the pleasure of meeting them. But Roger Moore stands out the most.

Approximately a year after assuming the role of Supervisory Inspector, I was given the opportunity to advance within the inspections program. I was appointed as the Area Port Director for the U.S. Virgin Islands, overseeing the ports of St. Thomas, St. Croix, and St. John.

Well, here I am again, heading back to Linda to ask for another move. Surprisingly, after hearing me out, she approved my plans for the USVI, and I was excited about the opportunity.

I completed my remaining tasks in Atlanta and bid everyone farewell.

Now, I'm on my way to the U.S. Virgin Islands. Not fully knowing what I was getting into, but I'm going anyway.

I thought hard about the opportunity, and many times I used to say to myself that I am right where the Lord wants me to be. So, if I am going to the U.S. Virgin Islands, then there must be a reason.

When you're right where God wants you to be, you will automatically know it. In Romans 12:2, it is said that when we offer our entire lives to Him to use as He desires, He'll reveal His will for us in return—his good, pleasing, and perfect will. So, going to the USVI is right where God wants me to be.

CHAPTER 16

Area Port Director

Earlier, I spoke about arriving in Marfa and experiencing a different kind of culture shock. Well, the U.S. Virgin Islands were another adjustment to make. Although I had been to St. Thomas for work before, I didn't have the chance to explore the island while there. I've traveled to many places and continents, and can tell you where to eat in any major city, but I've never had the opportunity to sightsee in any of these locations BECAUSE I WORKED!

For instance, one day, I flew from New Orleans to Los Angeles, Seattle, Minneapolis, and Detroit, conducting at least two or more interviews in each city. I completed this in one day. My only form of sightseeing was from the airport to the government offices and back to the airport, taking a different route.

Arriving in St. Thomas in April 2001 was a cultural shift for me, and I know it was for Linda as well. Remember, Linda had never been there before. I shared this story in my first book about Linda traveling there with our cat, "Sam." If you haven't read the first book, I NEVER SAW IT COMING, please do. While you are at it, please pick up the second book, I Was A Police Officer.

As the Area Port Director, my main office was located at Cyril E. King Airport in St. Thomas. I also had an office in St. John and in St. Croix. The United States Virgin Islands, comprising St. Thomas, St. Croix, and St. John, are among the most popular tourist destinations in the Caribbean.

On my first full day at work, I was setting up my office and trying to move in when everything seemed to hit me at once. Supervising the inspection program was easy, but adjusting to the arrival of foreign flights and their schedules was challenging. I also supervised the Examination Unit, which investigated cases involving visa fraud, marriage fraud, Naturalization Certificates, and Permanent Residence applications.

I supervised the Senior Inspector program, which was responsible for investigating and prosecuting cases stemming from airport inspections. The Detention and Deportation program was particularly challenging because it involved the deportation and custody of undocumented immigrants attempting to enter the USVI illegally. The Criminal Investigations Unit was well-organized and faced few issues.

However, managing the daily operations of cruise ships was my biggest challenge, and I'll share more about this later.

Everything I just said was from my first day on the job. I was handling these issues before I even got a chance to sit behind my desk. The back of my pants never hit the seat before I was putting out fires.

I had three supervisors in the inspections unit in St. Thomas and two supervisors for inspections in St. Croix. I also had a supervisor in the Detention and Deportation unit and the Exams unit. However, as the new port director, all the supervisors needed to understand how I wanted things done. To me, there was only one way to do things: do it right.

Requirements to enter the USVI

I was always asked the question, "Are passports required to travel to the United States Virgin Islands?" U.S. citizens do not need a passport to enter the U.S. Virgin Islands. Still, you need to show proof of citizenship (a raised-seal birth certificate and a valid government-issued ID card, such as a driver's license) when departing the U.S. Virgin Islands, including St. Thomas, St. Croix, and St. John.

Even though you are not required to have a passport to travel to the U.S. Virgin Islands, you may want to consider taking a passport instead of carrying the two forms of identification needed for departure from the U.S. Virgin Islands.

Island Time

The most frustrating thing I had to adapt to was "island time." That's right, everyone there on the islands, including the government workers, was on island time. For example, one day, I went to Burger King in St. Thomas for lunch. I walked in to order my meal, and I was the only customer there. I thought, well, this should be quick. I ordered a Whopper meal with a Coke; that was easy enough. I paid and stepped back to wait, all by myself.

Well, I waited and waited, but I didn't see any of the staff doing anything. They were standing around talking to one another. After about ten minutes, I stepped up to the counter and asked, "Excuse me, what's the status of my order?" One person looked at me and said they weren't going to make just one Whopper meal, and they were waiting for other orders so they could do them all at once.

As I was about to lose my temper, another customer came in and placed an order. He, too, ordered a Whopper sandwich. A few minutes later, I got my meal. The whole time there, the staff were friendly and very polite. To them, this was normal. From then on, I learned to relax, stay calm, and adopt the island's pace.

Managing all three islands required frequent travel. Weekly, I flew to St. Croix for a day or two to oversee operations. St. Croix was the only island where driving at 50 mph was possible. Both St. Croix and St. Thomas faced similar work-related challenges. St. John primarily served as a cruise ship port, but it also welcomed daily visitors from the British Virgin Islands, who came for day trips to shop or visit the island.

Cruise Ship Operations

The cruise ships arrive on the islands daily. In St. Thomas alone, during cruise season, four to six ships could dock at the port each day. In St. John, two to four ships might arrive, and in St. Croix, four to six. Additionally, several cargo ships arrive each day, making the inspection process a bit more challenging.

Each cruise ship had to be inspected by immigration inspectors, and usually it would take at least four inspectors per ship. Passengers and crew members were not allowed to go ashore until they had been properly cleared, and all passengers were required to present themselves and their documents to a U.S. Immigration Inspector before disembarking.

Each cruise ship had anywhere from 1800 passengers to larger ships with 5000 passengers. Crew members can range from 300 to 600 to be inspected. Crewmembers were permitted to enter the U.S. on a "crew list visa." A ship's agent or master obtains crew list visas from an American Consular Officer before the ship enters the United States.

Inspecting the cruise ships was reasonably straightforward. The vessel maintained proper documentation and ensured that all passengers had the necessary paperwork and up-to-date information. If any problems arose, they mainly involved crew members, but they were easy to resolve. If, for any reason, a crew member had an issue with documents or other matters and you refused them entry, they would not be allowed to disembark.

Inspecting U.S. citizens involved reviewing their U.S. passports. Inspecting foreign nationals involved reviewing their visitor's visa, specifically a B-2 visa, which allowed them to enter the U.S. from a foreign country and stay in the U.S. to visit. The B-2 visa allowed them to stay for up to six months as visitors.

Some days, there could be a stowaway on the ship that you would have to deal with. A stowaway is a person who secretly boards a ship. Sometimes, the purpose was to travel from one place to another without incurring transportation costs. In other cases, the goal was to enter another country without first obtaining a travel visa or other permission. Stowaways differ from people smugglers in that they need to avoid detection by the ship's crew and others responsible for the safe and secure operation of the cruise ship.

Several stowaways travelled by sea over the period I was there. Some stowaways had died during the attempt, especially on a cruise ship or cargo ship where they hid, because it was a dangerous place for them to hide. Sometimes they starved to death, and on occasion, if they were caught on cargo ships, they could be thrown overboard. That's correct; the captain of some of these foreign cargo ships did not want any confrontation with immigration at their next port, especially if they had something to hide on board.

Generally, the most challenging part of inspecting a cruise ship was the time it took to complete the inspection. It was time-consuming, but necessary. Every morning, around 5 a.m., I began carefully monitoring cruise ship operations and was ready to assist any supervisor as needed.

In St. Thomas, once ships were inspected and allowed to disembark, the town of Charlotte Amalie was filled with tourists all heading to the area of blue tents. It was called that because, down on the waterfront, there were many blue tents where locals sold their goods, such as shirts, trinkets, and a variety of items for tourists to purchase as souvenirs.

St. John became crowded once the ships were inspected. Most tourists in St. John go on diving tours and sailing trips around the island. Some catch the ferry and ride over to St. Thomas to go on tours.

When it came to St. Croix, it was similar to St. Thomas in terms of the number of tourists. Tourists also took diving tours, traveled around the island, and many people wanted to try some of the restaurants, especially those serving conch. Pronounced "konk", this seafood meat comes from an oversized sea snail and is native to the coasts of the Bahamas, the Florida Keys, the Caribbean, and Bermuda. It is generally served raw or cooked (fried), and it is very delicious.

Forty-Eight Chinese

On April 24, 2001, forty-eight illegal Chinese immigrants were detained and placed in federal custody after they entered St. John illegally.

I was later told that it was the largest roundup of undocumented Chinese nationals ever on St. John. The illegals were detained near Coral Bay and transported by federal and local authorities to the Immigration and Naturalization Service for processing on St. Thomas.

Since I arrived on the islands, there has been a rise in undocumented Chinese nationals arriving in the U.S. Virgin Islands. Recently, there had been an increase in incidents on St. John. This was likely due to the location, situated between the U.S. Virgin Islands and the British Virgin Islands. The ships entering the channel had islands on either side that they could retreat to in the event of an emergency. But their goal was to reach the U.S. side.

Processing large numbers of undocumented immigrants occurred almost every week. With the number of agents assigned to the islands, it sometimes took a toll on us. The following were several stories about illegal immigrants we encountered.

Thirty-six Chinese Nationals

One day, while attending to my regular duties, I received a phone call stating that thirty-six Chinese nationals had arrived on the shores of St. John illegally. That happened on May 18, 2001, when, early that Sunday morning, many citizens living on St. John started calling the police to report Chinese nationals arriving ashore near Coral Bay, and they were running away.

The St. John police responded to the calls around 6:30 a.m. and managed to detain thirty-six Chinese nationals by 8:30 a.m. I gathered my immigration investigators and inspectors, and we traveled to St. John to conduct the investigation.

We arrested all thirty-six Chinese nationals and transported them to our detention office on St. Thomas.

After officially processing the Chinese nationals, I arranged temporary housing at one of the island's detention facilities. Later, we transferred the Chinese citizens to San Juan, which involved flying them there. Eventually, the Chinese nationals were moved to one of the immigration detention centers in the United States.

While we were overseeing these thirty-six illegal Chinese nationals, we had just previously apprehended nine Haitian nationals being smuggled into Francis Bay, including one woman five months pregnant. Additionally, three days earlier, we apprehended thirty-three Chinese nationals at 2:00 a.m. coming ashore at Caneel Bay Resort in St. John. There were weeks when the immigration personnel working on the islands worked tirelessly to accomplish their mission, often with little sleep and rest.

Often, it was common to see two or three small boats arriving with illegal immigrants and foreign nationals rushing ashore at any given time. Sometimes, other boaters would give a heads-up to the Coast Guard, saying they saw a boat loaded with people miles offshore. The Coast Guard would contact us to inform us so we could prepare and prevent their escape when they arrived. We attempted to be at the location when they came to gather them, but the challenge was receiving multiple reports of boats arriving at different places simultaneously.

Sometimes, if we had enough time, we would contact the San Juan District Office, and they would send investigators to assist us in St. Thomas; however, that was not always possible.

The largest group of illegal immigrants that I encountered coming ashore was over 350 Haitians and Dominicans. Between processing, finding detention space, preparing prosecution cases, and arranging deportation hearings, these individuals became a significant burden for everyone. A great majority of these individuals wanted to apply for political asylum, which significantly increased the processing time.

I was proud of how everything was coming together on the islands, especially considering all the issues agents had faced before I arrived. I felt like I was making a positive difference, and things had improved somewhat, not for me, but for the employees working on the islands.

Six People Dead

It was July 15, 2001, sometime after midnight, the U.S. Coast Guard informed me that up to thirty undocumented Colombian and Haitian nationals had departed French St. Martin late on July 14 aboard a 31-foot powerboat. It was later determined that the boat was headed for somewhere in the U.S. Virgin Islands. It was intercepted that night by a U.S. Coast Guard cutter about twenty miles southeast of Virgin Gorda, British Virgin Islands.

After a brief chase with the Coast Guard, the 31-foot boat capsized, throwing all the passengers into the ocean around 1:00 a.m. on July 15. The Coast Guard crew rescued twenty of the immigrants, including an infant girl from Colombia, who was pulled from the water as she drifted away. Six deceased bodies were recovered from the water, and at least two other people are believed to have been lost at sea, including a small girl. Other passengers may have drowned as well, but we couldn't confirm that. The boat's owner was operating it when it capsized. The Coast Guard stated that they believe the boat was overloaded with too many people on board.

The Coast Guard reported that when coming upon the vessel, the weather became rough, and the waves increased, causing the boat to fill with water and eventually capsize. Sixteen of the Haitians managed to hold onto the boat or float nearby, but six were confirmed drowned because there were no life jackets on board when it capsized.

According to U.S. Immigration protocol, I responded to the Coast Guard cutter that night, which came within three miles of St. Thomas's shores. I was instructed to meet the St. Thomas Police Department at the seaport, and they would assist by transporting me to where the Coast Guard cutter was waiting.

When I arrived at the seaport, the police were waiting for me in their 20-foot aluminum boat. I looked at the boat and the officers, and before I could say anything, one of them assured me that it was a good boat and safe. I asked how we are all going to fit in this boat and bring back six bodies with us. I was told that only I and one officer would be going out in the boat. The center of the boat was an open area, and I realized that we could place the bodies there for transport back. The officers informed me that they had used the boat before for similar missions and had been successful in those endeavors.

All the boats assigned to the USVI were stationed in San Juan, and it would have taken hours for them to arrive and pick me up to go out to the cutter. So, I used what was readily available.

It was pouring rain that night, and as we left the seaport, the seas were getting rough, with waves ranging from 3 to 5 feet, making for a challenging ride. We started slowly, going through the Bay Area, but when we hit open water, the officer opened the throttle, and off we went. Waves were splashing in our faces, but it was raining anyway, so we were getting wet one way or another.

While we were probably safe in that 20-foot boat, we endured a long, stormy night that was quite unpleasant. I should also mention that the USVI police didn't have the most modern equipment, and this boat was a good example. I had brought a flashlight with me, but the boat had a big overhead light that was very bright. We had to turn it off on the way out to the cutter so the officer could steer the boat. At one point, the officer bragged about how bright the light was, and as he was demonstrating its operation, the light went out. We were never able to get it to work again. Thank God for my flashlight. The officer also had a flashlight, but it didn't work.

Our boat was powered by a 125-hp Yamaha engine that seemed on the verge of giving out. The officer accompanying me never hesitated and carried himself with complete confidence. I assume he was familiar with the boat and trusted its capabilities. Every time I glanced at him, he would be smiling broadly and giving me a thumbs-up. I must admit, it did help boost my confidence a bit.

When we arrived at the cutter, we tied up alongside. I boarded by climbing up a Jacob's ladder. A Jacob's ladder is a portable ladder made of rope and used primarily as an aid in boarding a ship, such as this cutter. I considered myself reasonably fit at the time, as I was working out and trying to stay in shape. When I reached the top of Jacob's Ladder and climbed aboard, I made a promise to myself to increase my workouts and get into better shape.

Once on board, I met with the captain and was able to view the six deceased bodies they recovered. I remember standing there, looking at the people who were rescued, of all ages. I looked at several small children sitting on the deck, shivering from being cold. They were drinking small cartons of milk and eating a cookie. Those poor children did not ask for any of this. Their eyes were as wide as they could be; they were scared, and I noticed them looking around, probably wondering what would happen to them next. Several were looking around for their family members, but they couldn't find them. Several were crying, and some Coast Guard members were attempting to console them. Those who didn't see their families looked scared while they sat there shaking. Several of the children stared at me as if I was there to save them somehow. When I came on board, several stood as if they wanted to walk toward me. They were seeking and needed help from someone, anyone. They were scared out of their wits.

As I looked at the adults standing near the children, I wondered why they weren't trying to help console the children. The USVI police officer spoke with several of the adults and asked them that question. They responded that they were not the child's guardian. So, they didn't care.

I did get a little upset with the Coast Guard that night because, as the six deceased bodies lay on the deck, they were close by where the children could view them. I asked the Coast Guard to remove the children and put them inside so we could put the bodies in body bags.

Seeing the children and knowing what they went through saddened me. I recall getting emotionally upset, actually mad at the adults who put those children through this. Of course, I understood that I couldn't let my emotions get ahead of me. I had to put all that aside now and collect the deceased bodies. But still, as I looked at those adult Haitians standing there, I considered charging each one of them for endangering the safety of the children. We also believed there was one female child who had been lost and had floated away before she could be rescued.

After loading the six bodies onto our boat, the weather worsened with rain, wind, and rough seas. At least the boat we were on was equipped for such a situation. We positioned the bodies in the center of the boat, shoved off from the cutter, and started our return to the St. Thomas seaport. The remaining people stayed on board the cutter to be transported to shore later that morning.

As the pouring rain continued, the wind intensified, and the waves grew rougher. I had a small rope and began tying the bodies together to keep them from being tossed out of the boat. When I say the water was rough, we had to go slow enough to stay with the waves and avoid being thrown around.

After a grueling ride, we made it back to the seaport. The coroner's office was there waiting for us to take possession of the bodies. I followed them to the morgue so that I could take photos of the bodies for evidence and start preparing all the necessary documentation for a criminal case.

At the morgue, the U.S. Immigration Investigations unit took control of the case. Immigration agents from St. Thomas, working in conjunction with the U.S. State Department and local police, conducted a thorough investigation. Interviews were undertaken later, and evidence was collected and prepared for forensic examination.

After a complete, thorough investigation, investigators arrested and charged two men with six counts each of alien smuggling resulting in death, as well as seventeen counts of alien smuggling endangering lives. One man was the owner of the boat that was carrying the Haitians.

On December 14, 2001, following the presentation of what appeared to be substantial evidence during the trial, a jury acquitted the two men from St. Thomas accused of causing the deaths of six individuals. They were found not guilty of six counts of alien smuggling that resulted in death and 17 counts of alien smuggling that endangered lives. If they had been convicted of causing the deaths of those six people, the two men could have faced life in prison.

During the three-day trial, the Assistant U.S. Attorney presented evidence that 30 undocumented Haitian immigrants left French St. Martin late on July 14th aboard the 31-foot powerboat owned by the St. Thomas native. They testified that the boat taking them to the U.S. Virgin Islands was intercepted that night by the U.S. Coast Guard cutter about 20 miles southeast of Virgin Gorda.

Testimony said that after a chase, their boat flipped over, tossing all of the passengers into the ocean. The Coast Guard testified that they saved the two owners and one crewman, as well as 17 of the immigrants, including an infant Colombian girl who was plucked from the water as she drifted away from the scene. Six bodies were pulled from the water, and at least two other people are thought to have been lost at sea, according to evidence presented at the trial. Different individuals from the boat might have drowned as well, but investigators have not been able to confirm that.

Trial documents revealed that the owner had registered the boat with the Planning and Natural Resources Department on St. Thomas only two days before the incident. Witnesses confirmed that the owner was the one piloting the boat that night.

The defense attorneys argued that no crime had taken place in the U.S. Virgin Islands and suggested that the boat may have capsized due to the wake of the Coast Guard cutter. They claimed that no one could prove the boat was headed for the U.S. Virgin Islands or that the aliens did not plan to report to immigration officials upon their arrival.

No one was ever convicted of the deaths of the six Haitians. So, their deaths were a wasted cause. After the trial, most of the witnesses on the boat were deported back to Haiti.

Honestly, I wasn't surprised considering the trial was held in St. Thomas. The islanders tend to look out for themselves. The boat owner was from the islands, but the deceased individuals weren't. This is just my opinion without proof, but I believe the islanders were unlikely to convict their own, especially concerning Haitians.

At least twice during the week, boats carrying undocumented immigrants reach the shores of the U.S. Virgin Islands, and they scatter everywhere, trying to blend into the community and avoid being caught.

Sometimes, we were fortunate, and fishermen who go 15-20 miles offshore may see a boat carrying more people than is safe, with no life jackets, and sometimes, some people hanging off the boat into the water, holding on for dear life. They report it to the U.S. Coast Guard, which may intercept the vessel or follow it to determine its intended destination, potentially for a beach landing. The Coast Guard only intervenes when the boat is approaching U.S. waters.

Several Coast Guard members once told me that smugglers were using a route that runs northwest along the Leeward Island chain and through the British Virgin Islands. It was challenging to choke off because the British Virgin Islands are only a mile away from the U.S. Virgin Islands, and the smugglers can blend in with the heavy tourist traffic on the boats.

Migrants usually fly to Dominica or nearby islands and then connect with smugglers who transport them on chartered boats under the cover of night to the U.S. Virgin Islands. When they land on the shores of the U.S. Virgin Islands, they attempt to sneak into nearby Puerto Rico by boat while some seek political asylum. Haitians would try to remain illegally in the U.S. Virgin Islands, which had a local Haitian community.

But those migrants would need false identification to pass immigration checkpoints at U.S. Virgin Islands airports. There are no checkpoints for passengers flying to the U.S. mainland from San Juan, but immigration would occasionally conduct random checks on passengers.

I read that the British Virgin Islands, once a pirates' stopover, have increasingly become a hub for Caribbean smugglers who use them to transport illegal migrants to the U.S. Virgin Islands and Puerto Rico.

Forty-eight Chinese Nationals

On October 22, 2001, we experienced an increase in Chinese nationals attempting to sneak into St. John illegally. After spending Sunday night stranded on the rocks east of St. John's Brown Bay, forty-eight illegal Chinese aliens were apprehended by the U.S.V.I. National Park Service on Monday morning. Four park police boats transported them to the U.S. Immigration office on St. Thomas for processing.

To get them off the rocks, they used a raft that was borrowed from the U.S. Coast Guard to transport them from the rocks to their boats. The U.S. Coast Guard boat was patrolling the area, and one of the park rangers had to enter the water to assist the Chinese aliens in boarding the raft.

One of the residents on St. John reported seeing a group of Chinese people on the rocks around 3:24 p.m. on Sunday. The area where they were had no access road, so the work had to be done by boat.

At that point, it was too dangerous to attempt to rescue the people from the rocks, so the 13 women and 35 men were forced to spend the night exposed on the rocks.

When they were rescued from the rocks, the Chinese men and women reported that they had eaten whelks and cacti, and drank soda from cans. Whelk is a sea snail with a spiral shell and tender meat.

Several people sustained minor foot injuries after stepping on spiny sea urchins on their way to shore. Sea urchins are small, spiny marine animals found in oceans. They inhabit both warm and cold waters, typically in shallow regions such as rock pools, coral reefs, or areas exposed to wave action.

During the investigation, we discovered a powerboat with twin 200-hp engines abandoned on the beach at Leinster Bay, which was possibly connected to the arrival of the Chinese vessel. Still, we were never able to establish that connection. It illustrates the significant amount of money involved in smuggling. There is a lot of money involved when you can leave a boat with two 200-hp motors and leave it on the beach.

St. John was the most popular spot in the U.S. Virgin Islands for dropping off illegal aliens. People from different countries often pay thousands of dollars for the trip, trying to reach the U.S. mainland from the territory.

It's worth noting that conducting interviews with individuals from the Dominican Republic, Haiti, Barbados, Cuba, Bonaire, Curacao, Grenada, Jamaica, Martinique, and Trinidad and Tobago, among others, was very challenging. The primary issue was their level of education, as some had never attended any form of schooling.

The second issue was their remarkable ability to deceive. They were skilled due to their upbringing in their country and the survival skills they developed. I won't go into much detail about this due to disclosure concerns, but trust me when I say that most of these people were very adept at convincing others to believe them. They rarely told the truth and often fabricated stories among themselves. It was natural for them.

They never quite understood how to tell the truth properly or how to lie convincingly; it was simply something they did naturally. The only way I could discern reality from deception was by observing their micro expressions, watching their facial expressions, and their reactions to questions.

As demonstrated by the stories I shared, we faced numerous instances of unauthorized entries to the islands. These incidents involved not only Chinese nationals but also individuals from various other countries attempting to gain entry. We did our best to address the challenge of undocumented immigration, focusing heavily on St. John, which we identified as a main entry point for migrants. We worked with the Virgin Islands Police and other federal partners to ensure community safety and legal compliance.

Political Asylum

Many undocumented immigrants, when apprehended, often claim political asylum. People seek political asylum when they fear for their safety or are facing persecution or oppression in their home country. They then attempt to move to another country, and if they are allowed to stay there, it is considered a form of political asylum.

People seeking asylum often claim they were victims of threats, physical harm, or violations of their human dignity, which they perceive as violations of their human rights.

When these individuals requested political asylum, they were processed and then eventually interviewed by asylum officers before appearing before an Immigration judge. Political asylum is a human right protected by Article 14 of the Universal Declaration of Human Rights and international human rights law. Every country that once ratified the United Nations Convention Relating to the Status of Refugees was required to admit eligible individuals.

A true asylum seeker is an individual who can demonstrate that they may encounter significant harm in their country of origin due to their religion, political beliefs, membership of social groups or activities, personal lifestyle, or sexual orientation.

People often mix up the idea of exiling someone from their home country with the concept of seeking political asylum; though, these are different ideas. While sometimes, people choose to migrate for personal reasons, which can be seen as a form of political migration, it's usually not something that the government initiates.

Those granted political asylum were referred to as refugees. They are often mistaken for "economic refugees," who move from a poor country to a richer one to work and earn more money, typically to support their families.

Gateway to the States

You must first understand why these individuals were attempting to enter the U.S. Virgin Islands (USVI) undetected. They were not all coming to live in St. Thomas, St. Croix, or St. John permanently. Their goal was to reach the USVI and blend into the community for a while. They want to eventually make it to the States or Puerto Rico to join up with a family member who is already established.

Please note I won't delve into all the details, but I will outline part of the process. After spending time on the islands without detection, they now need to obtain documentation to travel to the U.S. unless they can make it over to Puerto Rico. They may have to purchase a fake visa from a criminal source or attempt to acquire a counterfeit U.S. passport. This process incurs a substantial financial expense. Typically, a relative in the U.S. pays the fees without any certainty that the documents will be valid.

Understand that if they attempt to leave the USVI, they may be subject to presenting documentation to board an aircraft or ship to leave the USVI. If they can make it to Puerto Rico, then they need nothing but a form of identification to board an airline, even if it is fake.

If successful, they can reach the States and begin working to repay their relative. This was a brief overview. The process is much more complex than what was described, but that could fill another book.

Another challenge they faced was the people of the USVI. The islanders know who belongs there and can quickly identify outsiders. If this occurs, the illegal migrant often pays off an islander to stay silent. Usually, they lack financial resources, so they end up working for little or no pay, such as cleaning houses or working in a business to maintain their anonymity. As a result, their chances of reaching the States become very slim because they rarely earn money, and they fear being turned over to immigration authorities. Living in the USVI also feels safer than the country they left.

So, for years, they were stuck there, but in reality, some ended up being treated very well, working in islanders' homes. They have room and board, and eventually, they earn a little money. I met many people in these circumstances, and they became very happy with how things turned out. Besides, they never missed the States because they had never been there. You can't miss something you never had.

Understand that illegal migration was a serious problem in the USVI, where many illegal drugs and immigrants begin their entry into the United States. Before I arrived in St. Thomas, the USVI and Puerto Rico were classified as High Intensity Drug Trafficking Areas, a designation that remains today. The USVI served as the main point of drug flow, with countries like Venezuela, Colombia, and the Dominican Republic supplying drugs to these territories for local use or distribution onward to the mainland U.S.

Transporting narcotics through the USVI and Puerto Rico was relatively easy due to approximately a thousand miles of accessible entry points. These points restrict U.S. Immigration and Customs searches on domestic cargo passing through the territory. During my time there, a persistent issue in the USVI was illegal immigration of primarily criminal aliens. Human trafficking through the USVI was on a smaller scale than what was on the U.S.-Mexico border. In many cases, higher-profile illegal aliens, on average, who were members of international criminal organizations, were being trafficked to the U.S. mainland through the territory.

Chapter 17

My Two Cents

The United States attracts more international migrants than any other country for those seeking a new beginning abroad. It has traditionally served as a place for people to leave one country and move to another. People are motivated by the pursuit of opportunity and a desire to escape persecution, poverty, and famine. Immigrants come to America seeking freedom, employment, and a better life.

The United States is often referred to as "a nation of immigrants" and "a melting pot," because of its cultural diversity. The Statue of Liberty was usually the first sight immigrants saw upon arriving in America, as they disembarked at Ellis Island. There, they underwent inspection and formal processing. The statue's uplifted torch welcomed millions of immigrants. Migrants from Mexico and Central and South America have troubled many U.S. citizens because some of the immigrants entered the U.S. illegally without background checks for possible criminal histories.

While Americans' adverse reactions to immigration are often emphasized, it is recognized that many immigrants play roles in their communities. Whether documented or not, immigrants usually make significant contributions to the economy by paying taxes and enhancing the workforce.

A Path to Citizenship

Now, I might step on some toes, but the following is information for discussion.

The debate over whether the U.S. should create a pathway to citizenship for undocumented immigrants inside the country has become a heated discussion.

The path to citizenship would allow undocumented immigrants to become U.S. citizens. However, this process may involve additional fees, background checks, or extended waiting periods beyond those already required for legally documented immigrants.

Gaining citizenship grants immigrants access to government benefits, including Social Security, voting rights, family reunification, and protection from deportation, even if they have committed a crime.

Legalization

Legalization allows undocumented immigrants to stay in the country legally, but it does not grant them U.S. citizenship or the same rights as citizens. They would be permitted to work in the U.S., travel legally in and out of the country, and would not be subject to deportation for being present there (although committing certain crimes could still lead to deportation). They would not be able to vote, receive government benefits, or petition to bring family members into the country. Alternatives to citizenship and legalization include the deportation of undocumented immigrants.

Amnesty

Let's talk about amnesty. Amnesty is often viewed as a means to obtain citizenship and legal status. It functions like a pardon for individuals who have committed offenses against the U.S.

In immigration law, this refers to the government's forgiveness for individuals who use false or forged documents to seek employment and remain in the U.S. It might enable undocumented immigrants to obtain permanent residency, which could eventually lead to citizenship.

Undocumented immigrants from Mexico made up the largest group applying for amnesty.

Both Democratic and Republican presidents have supported, discussed, or implemented similar policies regarding a pathway to citizenship.

Pros and Cons

Below are some pros and cons associated with the pathway to citizenship. These observations and concerns are frequently articulated in nearly every discourse regarding the pathway to citizenship.

Pro: Undocumented immigrants have resided in the U.S. for many years, paying taxes, and therefore deserve a pathway to citizenship.

Con: Undocumented immigrants have violated laws that legal immigrants adhere to, and should not be granted citizenship.

Pro: Many undocumented immigrants arrived as children, had no alternative but to violate immigration laws, and are unfamiliar with other countries.

Con: The U.S. is required to enforce existing immigration laws.

Pro: The United States is both a country governed by laws and a nation built by immigrants.

Con: A pathway that falls short of granting citizenship—keeping families united without rewarding illegal residency—would be more humane and suitable for undocumented immigrants.

This is merely a point for your consideration. Once again, these were my reflections and my "two cents," regardless of their value.

New Orleans Supervisory Special Agent

My experience in the U.S. Virgin Islands was enjoyable and stimulating at times, offering valuable learning opportunities. Managing multiple departments helped me acquire new skills and develop innovative strategies to achieve my goals.

During my time there, I acquired many learning experiences that clarified my role within each department. These lessons gave me valuable insights and the essential tools to manage the job's complexities effectively.

When the opportunity for the Supervisory Special Agent position in New Orleans presented itself, I initially found the prospect quite challenging. After consulting with Linda and contemplating the situation, I subsequently felt sufficiently confident to submit my application.

In June 2002, I was selected for the position and transferred from St. Thomas to be a Supervisory Special Agent for U.S. Immigration in New Orleans. This will be covered in my next book, SPECIAL AGENT, coming out soon.

CHAPTER 18

Choosing A Career As A Federal Agent

Choosing a career as a federal agent can be an exciting and rewarding professional path to take. Federal agents enforce federal laws and investigate crimes under federal jurisdiction. Job opportunities are available in various government agencies.

The duties of a federal agent can vary depending on the agency for which you will work. Responsibilities may include conducting investigations, gathering evidence, making arrests, appearing in court, and collaborating with law enforcement agencies at local, state, and international levels. These duties can also involve dealing with drug trafficking, organized crime, terrorism, cybercrime, financial fraud, public corruption, human trafficking, and more. Agents handle complex cases that require detailed research, surveillance, and cooperation with other agencies.

The work environment can vary; you may be assigned to work in an office, conducting research and analyzing data, or in the field, conducting interviews and gathering crucial evidence in a case. Some agents may even take part in undercover operations or surveillance activities.

The workdays for an agent are long, and you may be on call around the clock. You must be prepared to respond to emergencies and assist other law enforcement teams when called on. The work is both physically and mentally demanding.

The education and training required to pursue a career as a federal agent can vary depending on the specific agency or department. Nevertheless, the majority of agencies stipulate a minimum of a bachelor's degree, such as in criminal justice. Certain agencies may also require prior law enforcement experience or specialized competencies. In some cases, college credits may be considered as a substitute for law enforcement experience.

Once hired, you will be required to attend training at the agency's academy, which includes both classroom instruction and practical exercises designed to develop essential skills and knowledge. They also must stay updated with the latest laws, investigative techniques, and technological advancements.

To be successful, you are expected to uphold the highest standards of integrity and ethics in your work. You must adhere to the law and maintain the confidentiality of sensitive information at all times. You will also need strong analytical and critical thinking skills. Keep in mind that working in federal law enforcement requires analytical thinking, physical stamina, and an unwavering commitment to justice.

Suppose you are preparing to seek a job with the federal government as a federal Agent. In that case, you must be ready to showcase not only your knowledge and skills but also your dedication to upholding the law.

In conclusion, a career as a federal agent can be gratifying for those interested in federal law enforcement. It requires dedication, commitment, and a strong sense of responsibility, as federal agents play a vital role in protecting public safety and upholding justice nationwide.

In my next book, SPECIAL AGENT, I will share my professional journey as a Special Agent for the U.S. Immigration and Naturalization Service (INS), subsequently transitioning to U.S. Immigration and Customs Enforcement (ICE), which culminated in my decision to retire.

I had the opportunity to supervise various investigative units, including the Criminal Alien Group and the Asset Forfeiture Unit.

Additionally, I discuss serving as a Section Chief at the Department of Homeland Security's Headquarters in Washington, D.C. and working as a Special Agent for the Department of Homeland Security Internal Affairs.

Keep an eye out for SPECIAL AGENT — arriving soon!

Please visit my website at www.authordonaldrsmith.com for updates.

www.ingramcontent.com/pod-product-compliance
Lightning Source LLC
Chambersburg PA
CBHW051315120626
46547CB00015B/2248